ETHICAL INTUITIONISM

W. D. HUDSON, M.A., B.D., Ph.D.

Reader in Moral Philosophy, University of Exeter

MACMILLAN

ST MARTIN'S PRESS

First edition 1967
Reprinted 1970

Published by
MACMILLAN AND CO LTD
London and Basingstoke
Associated companies in New York Toronto
Dublin Melbourne Johannesburg and Madras

Library of Congress catalog card no. 67-11400

SBN (paper) 333 05145 9

Printed in Great Britain by
RICHARD CLAY (THE CHAUCER PRESS), LTD
Bungay, Suffolk

CONTENTS

CONTENTS

PREFACE

New Studies in Ethics, to which series this volume belongs,
consists of monographs written by philosophers drawn from
universities in Great Britain, The United States, and Australia.
The series covers the main types of ethical theory from Greek
antiquity to the present day.

The present work deals with the view that men, as such, are
endowed with consciences which give them an immediate and
unerring awareness of moral values. Can this view be sustained?
What opinions have been held concerning the nature of conscience
and the content of its deliverances? Does it make sense to speak
of knowing by intuition right from wrong, good from evil?
Such questions are here discussed with particular reference to the
British philosophers of the seventeenth and eighteenth centuries,
who gave classical expression to ethical intuitionism.

I asked three friends, Professor D. J. O'Connor, Mrs. Pamela
Huby, and Mr. Peter Quartermaine, to read the typescript of this
study. I am most grateful for their comments which have, I hope,
helped me to make my meaning clearer at certain points. They bear
no responsibility for the defects which remain.

W. D. H.

I. INTRODUCTION

Ethical intuitionism is here taken to be the view that normal human beings have an immediate awareness of moral values. Our approach to the subject will be through a study of some of its classical exponents in British philosophy. Some of these have contended that the awareness in question can only be conceived satisfactorily as a form of sense-perception. Shaftesbury and Hutcheson will be our sources for this 'moral sense' view. Others have argued that it is his reason, or understanding, which gives man this awareness. As examples of this view, we shall take Cudworth, Clarke, Balguy, and Price. The working out of these two points of view — sometimes differentiated as sentimentalism and intellectualism, sometimes as aesthetic and rational intuitionism — and the debate between their respective adherents dominated moral philosophy in Britain throughout the eighteenth century. Because he seems to have occupied a bridge position between the two points of view, Butler will serve us as an additional source.

Anthony Ashley Cooper, third Earl of Shaftesbury (1671–1713), had his early education supervised by Locke, then went to Winchester, and eventually entered Parliament as a Whig. He did not return to Parliament after the dissolution of July 1698 because of ill health, but went to Holland for a year, where he found both the physical and intellectual climates much to his liking. Though no recluse, he did not play any prominent part in public life, his interests being mainly intellectual and literary. His *Enquiry Concerning Virtue or Merit* was first published in 1699.

Francis Hutcheson (1694–1746) published the works for which he is best known, and with which we shall be concerned, while residing in Dublin, where he had opened a private academy. They were *An Inquiry Concerning Moral Good and Evil* (1725), *An Essay on the Nature and Conduct of the Passions and Affections* (1728), and *Illustrations Upon the Moral Sense* (1728). In 1729 he returned to the University of Glasgow, at which he had been a student, and occupied the Chair of Moral Philosophy there until his death.

Ralph Cudworth (1617–88) held various academic and ecclesiastical appointments. He was Master of Clare Hall and Professor of Hebrew at Cambridge, and subsequently Master of Christ's College. He became leader of the Cambridge Platonists, a group of religious philosophers, who, compared with other controversialists of the time, were notable for their reasonableness and tolerance. Their approach to ethics finds its clearest statement in Cudworth's *Treatise on Eternal and Immutable Morality*, published posthumously in 1731.

Samuel Clarke (1675–1729) was rector of Drayton, near Norwich, and later of St. James's, Westminster. He was versed in Newtonian physics and published scientific work in addition to his extensive theological and philosophical writings. Highly esteemed in ecclesiastical, academic, and court circles, he was, on Newton's death, offered the lucrative post of Master of the Mint, but declined. He is best remembered for his Boyle Lectures, published in 1706 under the title *A Discourse Concerning the Being and Attributes of God, and Obligations of Natural Religion, Etc.*

John Balguy (1686–1748) was also an Anglican divine and became vicar of Northallerton. He wrote *The Foundation of Moral Goodness*, parts I and II (1728 and 1729), expressly to support the philosophy of Cudworth and Clarke against that of Hutcheson.

Richard Price (1723–91) was a Unitarian minister who earned renown as a mathematician and notoriety as a political radical. He was elected to a fellowship of the Royal Society for papers *Towards Solving a Problem in the Doctrine of Chances*. A published sermon of his, welcoming the storming of the Bastille, is said to have been 'the red flag that drew Burke into the arena'. His *Review of the Principal Questions and Difficulties in Morals* (1758) is probably the best statement of the case for rational intuitionism which has ever been written.

Joseph Butler (1692–1752) was born into a Dissenting family and educated at a Dissenting academy, but eventually he was ordained in the Church of England. He became preacher at the

Chapel of the Rolls and his famous *Fifteen Sermons*, published in 1726, were delivered there. *The Analogy of Religion*, his *magnum opus*, containing the appendix *Dissertation upon the Nature of Virtue*, appeared in 1736. In time he became Bishop of Bristol and then of Durham.

We shall not, of course, attempt an exhaustive exposition of the moral philosophy of the thinkers named, but simply a general critical introduction to eighteenth-century ethical intuitionism as expressed in the works referred to, making clear, so far as we can, what was held in common by our authors and where they differed. Though it is eighteenth-century intuitionism with which we shall be concerned, the subject is not of merely antiquarian philosophical interest. Substantially the same views as those of some, at any rate, of our authors have found scholarly champions in our own day.[1] And, at the level of popular moralising, many of the contentions of classical intuitionism are widely canvassed still. We shall try to discover what truth, if any, lies in them.

The intuitionism with which we are here concerned was developed in conscious opposition to Thomas Hobbes (1588–1679) and others, such as Mandeville (1670–1733), who shared the standpoint popularly called Hobbism. The relevant elements in this philosophy, for our purpose, are (i) a conception of human nature as essentially materialistic, deterministic, and egoistic; and (ii) a conception of morality as a device discovered by men for securing the maximum degree of self-preservation. It was against the felt scandal of such opinions as these that our authors took up their pens.

Even his most ardent critics would have admitted that Hobbes developed his views with remarkable clearness and honesty. Believing, as he did, that everything in the universe can be explained in terms of physical motion, he applied this principle to man's voluntary activity. Appetite and aversion are defined respectively as movements towards, and away from, physical objects, the 'small beginnings' of such motion constituting imagination. 'Good' and 'evil' signify respectively objects of appetite and aversion. Pleasure is the sense of good; pain, of evil. Deliberation is the alternate arising of appetite and aversion.

3

The will is 'the last appetite in deliberating'. The words 'good' and 'evil', said Hobbes, 'are ever used with relation to the person that useth them; there being nothing simply and absolutely so. . . .' All morality, that is to say, is relative to the varying appetites and aversions of societies or individuals.

It is difficult to reconcile with his materialism Hobbes's belief that man has the capacity to take a long view of his situation so that there occurs the desire for power to make sure of future goods. However, he consistently assumed that the fundamental motivation in human conduct is towards self-preservation. 'All men agree on this, that peace is a good.' Reason suggests conditions under which it may be secured and these constitute morality. One is the creation of a compact by which each man surrenders some of his power of self-determination on condition that others do the same: '. . . the definition of injustice is no other than the not performance of covenant.' Another is the existence of a sovereign power, authorised to enforce the terms of the compact and strong enough to do so: '. . . before the names of Just, and Unjust, can have place, there must be some coercive power to compel men equally to the performance of their covenants.'[2]

The intuitionists directed their attack at two points. The first was Hobbes's account of human nature. They claimed that this simply did not square with the empirical facts. Men are not exclusively self-interested. Benevolence and a sense of duty are elements in human nature as evident as the desire for self-preservation. Their second line of attack was on Hobbes's attempt to reduce moral to non-moral discourse. They showed where he had failed to carry this through consistently, and pointed out that it would have been logically impossible to effect such a reduction. We shall return to these two lines of attack in Sections II and III.

In the remainder of this introduction we shall consider the main point at issue between our authors and Hobbes, which can be expressed thus: in what sense is morality natural?[3] Hobbes employed a concept, the law of nature, with which moral and political philosophies had long been familiar, but he transformed it out of all recognition.[4] Traditionally, the law of nature had meant the moral law, or certain fundamental aspects of it, which ought to govern life in society. It was conceived to be objective and absolute. It found expression in common law and the pronouncements of the Church, to which men were deemed to have a right of appeal against, for example, the fiat of any particular sovereign. But Hobbes gave to the expression 'a law of nature' this quite different meaning: 'a precept, or general rule, found out by reason, by which a man is forbidden to do that which is destructive of his life, or taketh away the means of preserving the same; and to omit that by which he thinketh it may be best preserved.' Examples of particular laws of nature in Hobbes are showing gratitude to a benefactor, pardoning those who, having done wrong, repent, and submitting disputes to arbitration. Hobbes said that such laws of nature, or articles of peace, are 'immutable and eternal', but the ground of this objectivity was not, for him, that of ultimate moral reality but of natural fact. 'For it can never be that war shall preserve life, and peace destroy it.' As we have seen, he taught that it is obligatory to keep the laws of nature only where there is a sovereign powerful enough to ensure, by the promulgation and enforcement of positive law, that all within the given society observe them. So to have rendered its objectivity factual and its obligatoriness contingent upon positive law was indeed to have transmogrified the law of nature!

The authors with whom we are concerned attempted to rehabilitate morality as 'natural' in something akin to the sense which this word had had in moral philosophy before Hobbes. Some of them, Shaftesbury, Hutcheson, and Butler, seem to have thought it enough if they could show that human nature is definitively moral. Moral judgment and even morally good conduct, they claimed, are natural to man as man. Cudworth, Clarke, Balguy, and Price went further, and contended that in moral judgment men perceive distinctions which are natural in the sense that they belong to the very nature, or essence, not only of man but also of things. We shall deal more fully with these views in Section II.

II. MAN BENEVOLENT AND MORAL

The intuitionists' first line of attack on Hobbes was that men are motivated by benevolence as well as by self-love; and that they possess a moral faculty, which judges of acts or states of affairs and excites to action, aside from all considerations of self-interest. Their contention was that any objective investigation of the empirical evidence of human behaviour would substantiate these claims.

First, benevolence. Shaftesbury discovered three kinds of affections or motives in man: (i) those, such as love or sympathy, which are directed to the good of one's kind; (ii) those, such as resentment, desire for sexual pleasure, love of praise or ease, directed to the good of the self; and (iii) those, such as love of cruelty for its own sake or 'a sort of hatred of mankind and society . . . a habitual moroseness', directed neither to the good of self nor of one's kind, but only to the barbarous and moment-ary satisfaction which such affections may produce. It is signifi-cant that he described the first class of affections as 'natural' (the second are called 'self-affections', the third 'unnatural').[5] Hutcheson also believed that there was a 'determination of our nature to study the good of others; or some instinct, antecedent to all reason from interest, which influences us to the love of others'; and that this benevolence was capable of being 'in some degree extended to all mankind'.[6] Butler, in his turn, pointed to friendship, compassional, parental, or filial love, for each of which there seemed to him to be just as good evidence in human conduct as for self-love.[7]

The rational intuitionists were equally convinced that man is by nature benevolent. Clarke contended expressly against Hobbes that 'there is in all men a certain natural affection' for their dependants or intimates; and that they 'naturally desire' to en-large this circle until it includes the community of mankind.[8] Price and Balguy recognised 'kind determinations in our minds' which 'engage, assist and quicken' men.[9]

6

There are, however, two points of difference between Hutcheson and the rationalists. (i) The rationalists sharply differentiated the question, 'Is it our *duty* to be benevolent?' from 'Is man *in fact* sometimes moved to action by benevolence?' They answered the latter question in the affirmative but held that duty consists in being benevolent *because* one sees that one *ought* to be. Such 'rational benevolence' is distinct from mere 'instinctive benevolence'. Instinctive benevolence, just because it is so natural to man, may in fact diminish the virtue of an action. It requires less regard for rectitude to succour others when we are attached to them, for instance by family ties, than when we are not. Hutcheson was criticised for having failed to make this distinction clear. (ii) Benevolence is, according to the rationalists, natural to man, not simply in the sense that it is instinctive, but also *because* it is *rational*. Butler had recognised that reason is often necessary to guide benevolence, but Balguy insists upon the correct order of priorities: 'It would be improper and absurd to say that we hearken to reason for the sake of our fellow-creatures; but it is very just and proper to say that we oblige and serve our fellow-creatures because reason requires it.'[10] Reason, or understanding, which discovers the nature of things, discerns the virtue of benevolence. So, since man is a rational being, this virtue is in accordance *both* with the nature of things *and* with the nature of man. To quote Balguy again: 'Let it [sc. virtue] by all means be represented as natural to us; let it take its rise, and flow unalterably from the nature of men and things, and then it will appear not only natural but necessary. I mean necessary in itself, though not in respect of its votaries, as being the object of their free choice.'[11]

It was recognised, of course, that, from the Hobbesian side, it could be forcibly contended that what appears to be benevolence is really disguised selfishness. Is our real motive, in fact, desire for the pleasure which we derive from benevolence, or for some other advantage contingent upon the practice of it? Undoubtedly, our own pleasure or profit are sometimes involved in the welfare of others. In such cases, we may, with cool calculation, promote the latter for the sake of the former. But can this

7

be stretched to cover all cases of benevolence? Suppose, said Hutcheson, a man knows that he is to perish at the next moment. Does this make him indifferent to the well-being of others? Surely those who have resolved upon death for country or friends prove otherwise![12] Price asked if it is conceivable that, before we desire any object, we have to learn that some pleasure or profit will accrue to us from attaining it. Do we not sometimes desire objects just for their own sakes? Suppose we could enjoy the same degree of pleasure without such objects as fame, knowledge, or esteem, would that make us indifferent to them? Men do, of course, find satisfaction in the fulfilment of desire or the thought of such fulfilment. But, as both Butler and Price pointed out, such satisfaction must be distinguished from the object of desire. The fact that we are satisfied when the object of desire is attained does not prove that the only object of desire is our own pleasure or profit. As Butler, though not Price, seems to have recognised, the latter may indeed be objects of desire, but even then, the satisfaction of attaining these objects is distinguishable from the objects themselves. It is sophistry or confusion to suppose that, because achieving the object of desire always gives satisfaction, such satisfaction is itself always that object.[13]

Butler attacked in particular the Hobbesian view that benevolence is really desire for power over others. Hobbes had written: 'There can be no greater argument to a man, of his own power, than to find himself not only able to accomplish his own desires, but also to assist other men in theirs: and this is that conception wherein consisteth charity.'[14] If this is so, asked Butler, how can we explain the facts that: (i) men desire the good of another sometimes, even when they know themselves powerless to achieve it, and rejoice when a third party does so; (ii) they sometimes prefer to do good to one person rather than another, even though the power exercised in each case would be the same; (iii) they experience good will and cruelty as quite distinct motives, though, if the former were merely delight in power, it is difficult to see why, since the latter could presumably involve an equal exercise of power to the former.[15]

8

The intuitionists believed that man is not only benevolent by nature but also moral. To the moral faculty three functions may be attributed: perception of moral properties; approbation or disapprobation; and motivation, or excitement to action. It was not in dispute that the moral faculty fulfils the first two; it perceives, and approves of, virtue. But does it also move to action? The writers whom we are considering did not all say unequivocally that it does; and where they did say that, they do not always seem to have been quite clear about what it implied. Hutcheson, for instance, while attributing perception and approbation to the moral sense, seems to have regarded benevolence as the motive of morally good action; but too much should not be made of this because he did not differentiate the moral sense and benevolence very sharply from one another, at any rate in the *Inquiry*.[16] Cudworth, in one place, wrote: 'Mere speculative intellection . . . is not the . . . beginning of all actions in the soul, but . . . instinct and inclinations are the spring and source of life and activity whence ends are suggested to us that provoke and incite endeavours and awaken consultation towards the attainment of them';[17] but it would be contrary to his whole standpoint to deduce from this remark that he held a view, similar to Hume's, of reason as merely the slave of the passions, able to calculate ways and means but not to move to action.

The motive of conscious action is the thought of a desirable end. It is significant that all our authors shaped their conception of the moral faculty in the light of their views concerning which faculty apprehends ultimate ends. Because sense does so, some held, the moral faculty must be sense; because reason does so, others said, that must be the moral faculty. It would have been curious, indeed, if any of them had thought that a faculty which apprehends ultimate ends cannot move to action. So we must conclude that, whether conceived as sense or reason, the moral faculty was believed by the intuitionists to fulfil all three functions: perception, approbation, *and* motivation.

Some rationalists, however, were not as clear as they might have been about what the claim that it moves to action implies, if the moral faculty is reason. Balguy contended that 'the same necessity which compels men to assent to what is true forces them to approve what is right'. This presumably meant that such a statement as 'A says that X is right, but A does not approve of X' is a formal contradiction. We need not dispute that. But when Balguy goes on to argue that a man's very approbation is a 'sufficient reason' for his choosing to do a right action, the case is different. The statement, 'If A approves of X, then he will choose to do X', if it is true, is not true because to deny it is self-contradictory. It is logically possible to approve morally of an action, but not do it. The point is this: if, as our rationalist authors thought, a rational being, *qua* rational, has a 'superior' or 'real' affection leading him to practise virtue, reason must be more than simply a faculty which discovers the truth or falsity of propositions and the entailments between them. It must also be a kind of love or desire — to quote Butler, 'a perception of the heart' as well as 'a sentiment of the understanding'. There are indications that the rationalists recognised this. Price, for instance, echoes these words of Butler at one point.[18] And Professor J. A. Passmore has called attention to the phrase 'higher intellectual instinct', used in Cudworth's manuscripts to describe reason, and suggested that this implies that he thought of reason as a kind of love, particularly the love of moral excellence.[19] But the rationalists' overriding view seems to have been the inadmissible one that reason, conceived simply as a faculty which perceives necessary truth, carries us from the perception of the necessary truths of morality to the affection for virtue.

In the case of man's moral nature, as of his benevolence, some of the intuitionists were aware that sophisticated Hobbists might suggest plausible ways round their claims. Hutcheson[20] faced the question: may we not approve of virtue in ourselves or others because, virtue being always to the advantage of mankind and ourselves being part of that whole, virtue is always to our advantage? He countered this with considerations such as the following. We approve of morally good actions so distant from us in time and/or space that our own interest does not seem to be involved. To the suggestion that we project ourselves imaginatively into these distant circumstances and consider how we might have benefited by the action, he replied that, if imagined self-interest thus determines our approval of events, why do we not always approve of victorious armies or successful tyrants? Moreover, men do, in fact, sometimes approve of actions which are, in the clearest sense, disadvantageous to them, e.g. the justice of a sentence passed upon them. It is surely a jest to say that such men approve of the sentence because it is in the public interest and therefore in their own. But even if this were accepted, what would it prove? Only 'that reason and calm reflection may recommend to us, from self-interest, those actions, which at first view our moral sense determines us to admire, without considering this interest'.

Hutcheson appeals to common sense against Mandeville's view that rulers, perceiving certain types of men to be useful for the defence of the State, had persuaded their subjects 'by panegyrics and statues' to approve of such men as public-spirited and to imitate them. It is claiming something for panegyrics and statues, he said, to suppose that they could persuade essentially selfish people that others are public-spirited, and even more, that they could induce the selfish to behave in ways detrimental to their own advantage.

Is man's approval and practice of virtue, then, self-interested in the sense that it is motivated by desire for reward from God? Hutcheson replied that many who do not believe in God are honourable, generous, just, etc.; and that this view would not explain why we approve of the virtue of others for which we shall receive no reward. Moreover, is not this view self-stultifying? If our only conception of good is advantage to self, then to say that God is good is to say that he acts for his own advantage. Since he is independent of us, what reason could there be for supposing that this good God, i.e. this God who acts for his own advantage, would reward us for doing good, i.e. acting for ours?

Is virtue, then, self-interested in the sense that we are excited to it by desire for the pleasure which it gives? Hutcheson pointed out that it is often far from pleasurable. But even if accepted, this view would presuppose that we can perceive virtue antecedently to any ideas from the practice of it.

III. MORAL DISCOURSE *SUI GENERIS*

The eighteenth-century intuitionists tried to show that moral discourse is *sui generis* and cannot be reduced to non-moral without loss, or change, of meaning. This was their second line of attack on Hobbes. They charged him and other apparent 'naturalists', such as Locke, with using ethical terms in such a way as to 'import something different from what they will allow to be their only meaning'.[21]

For instance, Locke appears to have identified the meaning of moral goodness with conformity to the law of God.[22] But if 'good' or 'right' is so defined, to say that God's law is right or good is, as Hutcheson put it, 'an insignificant tautology, amounting to no more than this, "That God wills what he wills" '.[23] As Richard Price said, Locke would have detested the consequences of his definition.[24] The latter insisted that God has the right to rule us, and offered, as his ground, that God has 'goodness and wisdom to direct our actions to that which is best'. Now, he well knew that if certain definitions are given to ethical terms, some ethical propositions will be rendered vacuous. Against Herbert of Cherbury, he had argued that, if virtue means conformity to God's will and best worship means that which pleases, then the remark, 'Virtue is the best worship of God', will mean simply that God is pleased with what conforms to his will, and this, though not exactly a tautology, is, as Locke said, 'of very little use'.[25] He must have intended what he himself had to say about morality to amount to more than this. But if rightness and goodness are defined as conformity to God's law, Locke's own remark, that God has the right to rule us because he has the goodness to direct our actions to what is best, is of even less use. All it tells us is that God's law is in conformity with his law because he conforms to his law in directing our actions in conformity with his law! Locke certainly meant something different from what his definition here of moral goodness would allow to be the only meaning of his words.

Hobbes, the main target of criticism, had said that obligation and all moral distinctions are constituted by compact. If so, then antecedently to such compact all actions and states of affairs are morally neutral. Clarke called attention to Hobbes's failure to recognise this. The latter had said that, prior to compact, there is a 'right of nature' whereby each man has 'liberty . . . to use his own power, as he will himself, for the preservation of his own nature; that is to say, of his own life'. How, asked Clarke, can that be reconciled with the view that the compact constitutes morality?

Again, Hobbes said that, at the compact, men lay down this '*right* of nature', or rather surrender it to each other, and then it can be said that each man is 'obliged or bound, not to hinder those, to whom such right is granted, or abandoned, from the benefit of it; and that he ought and it is his duty, not to make void that voluntary act of his own; and that such hindrance is injustice, an injury, as being *sine jure*, the right being renounced, or transferred'. If Hobbes had intended a non-moral 'ought' here, there would be no ground for criticism. His point would have been simply that, if the social compact is a necessary or sufficient condition of self-preservation, and if men wish to secure the latter, they ought to make and keep the compact. But it seems clear from Hobbes's language (which couples 'obliged' and 'ought' with words like 'duty', 'injustice', 'justice', 'right') that he intended a moral 'ought' here.

Hobbes's point was that the compact creates moral obligation. Now, the latter may be either hypothetical or categorical. And Clarke's criticism can be related to either alternative. If the obligation is hypothetical, it presupposes an end, independent of it, which has moral value, positive or negative. Clarke attributed to Hobbes the view that men ought to keep the compact in order to avoid the destruction of mankind. Such a view presupposes the negative moral value of this destruction and so is 'directly contradictory to Mr. Hobbes's first supposition, of there being no natural and absolute difference between good and evil, just and unjust, antecedent to positive compact'. If, on the other hand, Hobbes's 'ought' is taken to be categorical, he had, in the words of Clarke, 'no way to show how compacts themselves come to be obligatory, but by inconsistently owning an eternal original fitness in the thing itself'. The point here is that 'X ought to be kept' cannot be deduced from 'X is a compact' alone. The antecedent moral principle, 'All compacts ought to be kept' is a necessary additional premiss.[26] The same kind of criticism is to be found in Cudworth and Price.[27]

Professor A. N. Prior calls attention to the similarity between the eighteenth-century intuitionists' treatment of these attempts to reduce ethical language to non-ethical and G. E. Moore's discussion of 'the naturalistic fallacy'.[28] As Prior says, the similarity is most marked in the case of Richard Price. Price wrote: 'As to the schemes which found morality on self-love, on positive laws and compacts, or the Divine will; they must either mean, that moral good and evil are only other words for advantageous and disadvantageous, willed or forbidden. Or they relate to a very different question; that is, not to the question, what is the nature and true account of virtue; but, what is the subject matter of it.' This parallels Moore's distinction between a definition of an ethical term and a significant ethical generalization. The point is that to say, for instance, ' "right" means "conformable to the will of God" ' is different from saying, 'whatever conforms to the will of God is right.'

Price continues: 'Right and wrong when applied to actions which are commanded or forbidden by the will of God, or that produce good or harm, do not signify merely, that such actions are commanded or forbidden, or that they are useful or hurtful, but a sentiment concerning them and our consequent approbation or disapprobation of the performance of them. Were not this true, it would be palpably absurd in any case to ask, whether it is right to obey a command or wrong to disobey it; and the propositions, obeying a command is right, or producing happiness is right, would be most trifling, as expressing no more than that obeying a command, is obeying a command, or producing happiness, is producing happiness.'[29] If, in other words, by 'right' we mean X, then (i) the question 'Is X right?' is 'palpably absurd' because it means only 'Is X X?'; and (ii) the statement 'X is right' is 'most trifling' ('most triflingly identical' in Price's first edition) because it means merely 'X is X'. It seemed to Price necessary only to indicate these consequences of giving non-ethical definitions to ethical terms in order to show the logical impossibility of so doing. Moore is somewhat more explicit to the same effect. Whatever non-ethical definition (NED) we give to an ethical term (ET), 'we understand very well what is meant by doubting' that NED is ET and this 'shows clearly that we have two different notions before our minds'. Again, 'when [men] say "pleasure is good" we cannot believe that they merely mean "pleasure is pleasure" and nothing more than that'.

The argument with which some of the intuitionists with whom we are concerned attempted to refute all claims to reduce ethical to non-ethical language has, however, been turned against them. This began to happen even in the eighteenth century. Hutcheson realised that, on his 'moral sense' view, our moral judgments could conceivably have been other than they are. God might have made us with a moral sense different from that which we possess, e.g. one which approved of selfishness and disapproved of altruism. This is logically possible and so must lie within the power of an omnipotent being. It seems to follow that the moral distinctions which we draw are not absolute. Hutcheson found this apparent implication of his view uncongenial and tried to dispose of it. He argued that God has 'something of a superior kind, analogous to our moral sense, essential to him'; and that it would have been self-defeating if he had not made our moral sense in line with this: '. . . if the Deity be really benevolent, or delights in the happiness of others, he could not rationally act otherwise, or give us a moral sense upon another foundation, without contradicting his own benevolent intentions.'[30] But if the changelessness of morality is thus secured by appeal to the unchanging 'something . . . analogous to our moral sense' in God, then moral terms can have no referent, and so (if we accept for the moment the view that the meaning of a term is its referent) no meaning, which is independent of God's moral disposition or affections. This has disastrous consequences. Balguy showed why. 'I ask then. . . . Is such a disposition perfection in the Deity, or is it not? Is it better than a contrary, or than any other disposition would have been . . .?' This question seemed to him clearly not self-answering. Balguy expressed surprise that Hutcheson, while recognising that 'God's laws are just' is not an insignificant tautology, failed to see that 'God's disposition is good (or perfect)' is not one either: '. . . moral goodness no more depends originally on affections and dispositions, than it does on laws; and . . . there is something in actions, absolutely good, antecedent to both.'[31] There is, that is to say, a meaning to moral terms which is logically distinct from conformity to God's 'something of a superior kind analogous to our moral sense'. Thus the argument was turned against the 'moral sense' philosophers.

How has it been turned against their rationalist opponents? If the meaning of a word is its referent, and if moral language has its own distinctive and independent meaning, then moral words must have their own distinctive and independent referents. The rationalists saw this. So they contended that moral distinctions are 'founded in the nature of things', and claimed that these referents are known by rational intuition. In the sequel we shall argue that this latter claim cannot be sustained. But the point to notice at the moment is that the rationalists' view hinged upon the understanding of meaning as referent. Much recent moral philosophy has been influenced by the now prevailing view of meaning as use in the language.[32] The question asked, concerning meaning, has been not 'To what does moral language refer?' but 'What jobs do moral words do and under what conditions is it proper to use them for these jobs?' The kind of answer given has been: '. . . to express tastes and preferences, to express decisions and choices, to criticise, grade and evaluate, to advise, admonish, warn, persuade and dissuade, to praise, encourage and reprove, to promulgate and draw attention to rules; and doubtless for other purposes also.'[33]

Now, eighteenth-century rationalists took moral judgments such as 'it is morally fitting, or right, to show gratitude to a

16

benefactor' to state *facts*, albeit of a logically distinct kind; and they believed that it followed self-evidently, from the fact that an act would be morally fitting, or right, that it *ought* to be done. Balguy, for instance, said that to be under an obligation means to perceive some good reasons for acting, and 'if this moral fitness of certain actions be not a reason for the doing of them, I see not how anything can be a reason for anything'.[34] If X is fit, then X ought to be done. It has been argued recently against this view that, even if the fact that X is fit is called a 'non-natural' fact, all the objections to the naturalistic fallacy apply against it. If we so define moral terms, such as 'right' or 'good', that moral judgments become equivalent to statements of fact, we make it logically impossible for them to do their job of commendation. As Mr. R. M. Hare writes: 'If "P is a good picture" is held to mean the same as "P is a picture and P is C", then it will become impossible to commend pictures for being C; it will be possible only to say that they are C. It is important to realise that this difficulty has nothing to do with the particular example that I have chosen. It is not because we have chosen the wrong defining characteristics; it is because, whatever defining characteristics we choose, this objection arises, that we can no longer commend an object for possessing those characteristics.' The same applies to the use of 'good', or any other term, in a moral sense.

On this view, the statement 'If X is morally fit, then X ought to be done' is either an insignificant tautology or a *non sequitur*. If 'is morally fit' is defined as simply an odd way of saying 'ought to be done', then the statement is trivially analytic. If it is not so defined, then the statement fallaciously deduces 'ought' from 'is'.[35]

IV. MORAL SENSE

Shaftesbury attributed to man, as distinct from other sensible creatures, a 'natural moral sense'. He said that actions flowing from certain affections, or these affections themselves — such as pity, kindness, gratitude, and their contraries — being brought into the mind by reflection become objects and 'there arises another kind of affection towards those very affections'. We sense the beauty of some of these objects of thought and the deformity of others, just as we sense harmony or disharmony in colours or sounds. Virtue is beauty in the sphere of the affections; vice, ugliness. Virtue, that is to say, consists in a certain harmony or balance between self-affections and natural affections. A kind affection, such as generosity, tempered by sufficient self-affection to ensure the achievement of both private happiness and public good, constitutes virtue. The moral, or affective, sense reacts to this harmony, or the lack of it. This sense cannot be immediately or directly masked, but it can be corrupted by dissolute conduct or false religion. It will be seen that the moral sense, as Shaftesbury thus conceived of it, is not very clearly distinguished, if at all, from a sense of natural beauty.[36]

Hutcheson brought out more sharply the distinctiveness of the moral sense. He appealed to introspection. When men consult their own breasts, they find that they are affected in a distinctive way by what is morally good or evil. If, for instance, they are helped by generous friends, or see others so helped, they 'sense' such actions quite differently from assistance motivated by self-interest, or from mere good fortune. Hutcheson defined the moral sense thus: 'We must . . . certainly have other perceptions of moral actions than those of advantage: and that power of receiving these perceptions may be called a moral sense, since the definition [sc. of 'sense'] agrees to it, viz. a determination of the

18

mind, to receive any idea from the presence of an object which occurs to us, independent on our will.'

The 'moral sense' philosophers believed that the moral faculty must be a sense because their presuppositions were those of Locke's empiricist epistemology. Locke had taught that the ultimate, irreducible materials of thinking are simple ideas supplied by sensation or reflection. External objects are apprehended by the former, the operations of our own minds by the latter. Moral ideas seemed to Hutcheson to be 'simple ideas' in Locke's sense and, that which gave rise to them being objective, he deduced that they must be received through some form of, or something like, sensation. He drew out this analogy between our power of receiving the distinct perceptions of moral good or evil and our physical sense. Moral perceptions are as immediate as those of colour or taste. We do not deliberate, least of all as to how our own interests will be served, before we approve of generosity or disapprove of cruelty. The moral sense is like other senses in that it cannot be masked by self-interest. We may from motives of self-interest do an immoral act, but these motives 'have no more influence upon us to make us approve it than a physician's advice has to make a nauseous potion pleasant to the taste'. Hutcheson recognised that our moral faculty may represent its objects sometimes as they really are, sometimes otherwise, just as 'a sickly palate may dislike grateful food, or a vitiated sight misrepresent colours or dimensions'. But, he asked, since no one supposes from the latter that it is reason, not sense, which discerns the qualities of material objects, why should we conclude from the former that the faculty which perceives moral properties is not a sense?

He said that if the perceptions of our moral sense become disordered, they must be corrected, as are the perceptions of a sufferer from jaundice, by appeal to 'our ordinary perceptions, or those of others in good health'. This latter phrase 'in good health' appears to mean simply that the moral perceptions of those so described are in accordance with the judgments of the majority of mankind. But we do not, in fact, take it for granted that when a man's moral judgments place him in a minority, even of one, his moral sense is necessarily disordered or mistaken. Hutcheson took his analogy with physical sense to exclude the alternative possibility that 'in good health', in the case of the moral sense, means 'morally good'. He wrote: '. . . none can apply moral attributes to the very faculty of perceiving moral qualities; or call his moral sense morally good or evil, any more than he calls the power of tasting, sweet or bitter; or of seeing, straight or crooked, white or black.'[37] But, in reply, Adam Smith pointed out that we do apply moral attributes to the moral sense; if anyone approved of cruelty or disapproved of equity, we should not simply say that his moral sense was inconvenient to him, or his community, but that it was vicious and morally evil.[38]

Hutcheson might have countered this by calling attention to the fact that he had spoken only of a man pronouncing his *own* moral sense good or evil. There are indeed special difficulties about this. On Hutcheson's account of moral judgment, the moral sense, as subject, receives the idea of the moral value of the object being judged. It is logically impossible for the same moral sense to be both subject and object of such a judgment. My moral sense could conceivably receive the idea of the moral evil of judgments which I have made in the past, and, in this sense, I could disapprove morally of my own moral sense. But every moral judgment, on Hutcheson's view, presupposes a receiving subject, logically distinct from the object of the judgment, and so any man's own moral sense is systematically elusive to his own moral approval or disapproval.

There are two comments to be made here. (i) The first is the obvious one that this moral sense, to which moral attributes cannot be applied, is a necessary entity only on Hutcheson's presuppositions. If moral judgment is defined, not as the reception of an idea, but as an evaluation, then any matter of fact, even the fact that one's moral disposition is such and such, can logically be the subject of this evaluation. (ii) The second comment is that, if we were to substitute for the faculty of moral sense the concept of moral value, there would be some force in Hutcheson's observation. This concept is constitutive of the conceptual scheme of morality. One may accept it and think morally; or reject it and refuse to do so. What one cannot (logically) do is ask certain questions about the concept of moral value — for instance, the question 'What moral value has the *concept* of moral value?' Suppose A professes to think that it has none; B that it has some. In order to consider the question at all both A and B must (logically) accept the conceptual scheme of morality. A's answer, however, in effect rejects it, which is self-contradictory; and B's accepts it, which is tautologous.

Hutcheson admits that the moral sense is 'no doubt an occult quality'. The 'occultness' which he had in mind appears to be the fact that there are no physical organs of moral sense as of other senses. He asks: '. . . is it any way more mysterious that the idea of an action should raise esteem, or contempt, than that the motion, or tearing of flesh should give pleasure, or pain; or the act of volition should move flesh and bones?' The fact that we have bodily organs of sense such as sight or taste does not, says Hutcheson, solve the problem of how the mind is related to the body, but merely puts it one stage further back; and so, even though we have no bodily organs of moral sense, the physical senses are 'equally a mystery' with it.[39] This is a curious argument. What it amounts to, in effect, is that we need not worry about the problem of how we can have a moral sense, analogous to physical sense, when there are no apparent bodily organs of the former, because, even if we had such organs and so this problem did not exist, another problem would exist!

In the definition of the moral sense at the beginning of this Section, Hutcheson spoke of it as a 'determination of the mind to receive any idea from the presence of an object which occurs to us, independent of our will'. Professor D. D. Raphael has commented that this 'begs the question whether the moral faculty be sense or rational intuition'. He goes on: 'The criterion for using the name of sense is that the appearance of the objects of the faculty so named is not to be dependent on the exercise of the will, but is to be determined by causes external to us or implanted in our nature. Such a criterion would justify the use of the word "sense" for our rational faculties too; if I apprehend the equality of $2 + 2$ and 4 or the conclusion of a deductive inference, what I apprehend or intuit is not dependent on my will but is due to a necessary connection in or between the propositions considered. Of course I can choose not to consider the proposition at all, but I can equally choose to shut my eyes.'[40] Hutcheson's eighteenth-century opponents did not dispute that moral qualities are objective and apprehended by a faculty independent of the will, but they believed that there were grounds for comparing it to Cartesian intuition, rather than Lockeian sensation.

V. RATIONAL INTUITIONISM

Cudworth, Clarke, Balguy, and Price took the faculty which forms moral judgments to be reason or understanding. They accepted Locke's teaching that it is the work of the understanding to perceive agreements or disagreements between our ideas and that these relations constitute knowledge; and they contended that moral judgments are one aspect of such perception. It seemed to them as unnecessary to invoke a moral sense to explain our perception of this moral agreement or disagreement as it would have been to invoke an intellectual sense to explain how we perceive the agreement between the three angles of a triangle and two right angles.[41] In the words of Clarke: '. . . that there is a fitness or suitableness of certain circumstances to certain persons and an insuitableness of others . . .; also that from the different relations of different persons one to another, there necessarily arises a fitness or unfitness of certain manners of behaviour of some persons towards others, is as manifest, as that the properties which flow from the essences of different mathematical figures have different congruities or incongruities between themselves. . . .' He gave as examples of this moral fitness: '. . . 'tis . . . certainly fit that men should honour and worship, obey and imitate God'; and '. . . 'tis undeniably more fit, absolutely and in the nature of the thing itself, that all men should endeavour to promote the universal good and welfare of all, than that all men should be continually contriving the ruin and destruction of all.'[42]

It was this view of which Hume said that its authors, wishing to show that morality is demonstrable and discovered by reason, had simply assumed that virtue and vice must be relations, without making it at all clear what these relations were. Using the examples of a sapling overtopping its parent tree, and an animal committing incest, he argued that, whatever relation we were to propose as constituting virtue or vice, it could conceivably hold, not only between men but also between material objects or non-human creatures. Since we do not consider these to be 'susceptible of the same morality' as ourselves, it must therefore be a mistake to regard the essence of such morality as lying in relations.[43] We shall return to this consideration.

The rationalists all recognised that moral fitness or unfitness cannot plausibly be represented except as a specific kind of agreement or disagreement between ideas, distinct from all other kinds. Clarke, as we have seen, spoke of it as *absolute* fitness or unfitness, but there are difficulties in this conception. Selby-Bigge commented, in his introduction to *British Moralists*, that 'absolute fitness' is a contradiction in terms. He said that moral fitness must mean either fitness of a means to an end, or an action to a standard; and his point was that, though this end and standard may, indeed must, have moral value, neither can intelligibly be described as fit without some further end or standard being implied.[44] In other words, we cannot reduce morality to the mere concepts of fit or unfit. Among our authors, Price was alive to this. He wrote: '. . . agreement and disagreement, congruity and incongruity between actions and relations. These expressions are of no use, and have little meaning, if considered as intended to define virtue; for they evidently presuppose it.' In given circumstances, some actions have positive, others negative, moral value, and thus we come to speak of suiting actions to circumstances. But this and kindred expressions are 'only different phrases for *right* and *wrong* . . .'.[45]

Cudworth and his successors have been styled Platonists; but their debt was as great, if not greater, to Descartes. They believed that specifically moral agreements and disagreements between ideas are known by Cartesian intuition. Again, this view is represented most clearly in Price. His sentence from which we have just quoted continues: 'and it is to be wished that those who have made use of them [sc. these different phrases for right and wrong] had . . . avoided the ambiguity and confusion arising from seeming to deny an immediate perception of morality. . . .' Price differentiated two acts of the understanding: *deduction* (under

24

which head he included what we call induction as well as deduction) and *intuition*. He defined the latter as 'a power of immediate perception which gives rise to new original ideas'. These ideas or intuitions are 'simple and undeniable', i.e. logically irreducible and self-evident to rational beings, *qua* rational. He wrote: 'The various kinds of agreement and disagreement between our ideas, which Mr. Locke says, it is its [sc. the understanding's] office to discover and trace, are so many new simple ideas, obtained by its discernment. Thus: when it considers the two angles made by a right line, standing in any direction on another, and perceives the *agreement* between them and two right angles; what is this *agreement* besides their equality? And is not the idea of this equality a new simple idea, acquired by the understanding, wholly different from that of the two angles compared, and denoting self-evident truth?' But not only mathematical ideas: logical ones (such as necessity or identity), concepts in physics (such as solidity), metaphysical notions (such as substance or cause) and moral ideas (such as right, fit, good, obligatory) are also intuitions of the understanding on this view. They are all examples of what Descartes called 'clear and distinct ideas'. They shine by their own light. Without them all reasoning would be impossible. To them the last appeal is always made. They are the ultimate constituents of knowledge.

This Cartesian approach led our authors to two conclusions: (i) that just as geometrical proof is constituted by appeals to what is axiomatic, moral reasoning, where valid, breaks down into intuitions, such as that it is right to keep a promise; and (ii) that in such self-evident moral ideas we necessarily apprehend the nature or essence of things, for we cannot logically have any grounds for doubting that what self-evidently appears to be the case really is the case.[46]

There are two distinctions which are not clearly drawn here, but on which everything depends. (i) The first is that between the psychological and logical senses of 'self-evident'. Price asked whether we are not just as 'sure' of rightness in some actions as of equality in some mathematical figures. Now, it is one thing to feel sure that X is the case, but another to be able to show that it would be self-contradictory to deny that X is the case. We may indeed *feel* just as sure of a moral judgment as of a mathematical proof. But have we the same *logical* ground for doing so? When Price says, 'Do you not really know, that you are not deceived, when you think, that if equals are taken from equals, the remainders will be equal?',[47] the answer 'Yes' is guaranteed by the definition of 'equal(s)'. If we answered 'No' we should, in effect, be affirming and denying that they are equals. But it is, to say the least, by no means so clear that to answer the question 'Ought one to keep a promise?' in the negative is tantamount to saying that a promise is not a promise.[48] (ii) The other distinction is that between necessary and existential propositions. The logical necessity of '. . . if equals are taken from equals, their remainders will be equal' is undeniable; but there are objections to representing it as a necessity in the nature of things, an existent necessity. We have seen that the logical necessity is undeniable because it follows from the definition of 'equal(s)'. But this simply tells us something about the word 'equal(s)', given a certain definition and consistent usage. It tells us nothing about existence beyond that. There is an even more formidable objection to the concept of necessary existence, or existent necessity. Hume argued that this concept is self-contradictory. No proposition is logically necessary unless its denial is self-contradictory. But whatever we can conceive of as existent, we can also conceive of as non-existent. So, if existential, a proposition can be denied without self-contradiction. Therefore a proposition cannot be both necessary and existential.[49]

There are two distinguishable conceptions of moral fitness which are consistent with the view that it is known by Cartesian intuition. One is that which we have hitherto attributed to our authors, namely, that moral fitness is a *relation* between acts and situations or persons. The other is the view that the moral fitness of actions in situations is a property *entailed* by certain of their non-moral properties. According to the former conception, moral fitness is analogous to mathematical equality; according to the latter, to the equilaterality which is entailed by equiangularity in triangles. These two conceptions do not appear to be mutually exclusive. Some recent rational intuitionists have held to both. Sir David Ross, for instance, seemed to find no difficulty in speaking of rightness as fitness in a unique and indefinable way of actions to situations (i.e. a relation), while also holding the view that it is a 'consequential' characteristic of actions in situations entailed by such 'constitutive' characteristics as being the fulfilment of a promise.[50]

Is the latter view found in our authors? Raphael finds the view that moral fitness is an entailment as well as a relation in Clarke, whom he interprets as follows: 'In fact the relation referred to by Samuel Clarke has nothing to do with means and ends. For example in the situation "A is aware that B is in pain" there is a moral relation between A and B which can be expressed by saying "It is fitting for A to help B" or by saying "A is under an obligation to help B". (I myself do not find the first form of expression as satisfactory as the second.) This *relation* arises from elements in the existing situation, that is, from the facts that B is in pain and that A knows it. It does not arise from a possible future situation which does not now exist. Means and ends, causes and probable effects, have nothing to do with this relation; it is logically *entailed* by the existing situation.'[51] If Raphael is right, then Clarke and perhaps the rest of our rationalist authors thought of moral fitness as *both* a relation *and* an entailed characteristic.

The advantage of this view is that it would allow of a defence against Hume's criticism noted above. This was that whatever relation we propose as constituting virtue or vice, it could conceivably hold between things or animals as well as persons. Now if we say simply that a relation, e.g. incest, is immoral, then Hume may indeed ask, 'Why not then between animals?' But if morality is a matter of intuitive entailments, then it is permissible to reply that this relation is *only* intuited where persons are concerned. It is not the relation as such which is moral or immoral. The morality of the action is consequential upon certain constitutive characteristics of the action and the situation in which it ought to be performed, one of which is that *persons* are concerned. To the question, 'Why is the intuition so restricted?', the intuitionist has no answer except 'Because it is'. But this answer would not have embarrassed the rational intuitionists. Given their presupposition, that there are intuitions which do not require any justification beyond themselves, the reply is, of course, unexceptionable.

VI. BUTLER'S VIEW OF CONSCIENCE

Butler was influenced by both the rational intuitionists and the 'moral sense' school, and his account of the moral faculty has the appearance of a compromise, or an attempt at reconciliation, between their respective views. He speaks of the moral faculty as 'our moral understanding and moral sense'.[52] He argues that the existence of moral terms like 'right' and 'wrong' in all languages, and their universal use to distinguish, for instance, between injury and just punishment, presuppose 'a moral faculty; whether called conscience, moral reason, moral sense, or divine reason; whether considered as a sentiment of the understanding, or as a perception of the heart; or, which seems the truth, as including both'.[53] This is how he defines conscience: '. . . there is a superior principle of reflection or conscience in every man, which distinguishes between the internal principles of his heart, as well as his external actions; which passes judgment upon himself and them; pronounces determinately some actions to be in themselves just, right, good; others to be in themselves evil, wrong, unjust; which, without being consulted, without being advised with, magisterially exerts itself, and approves or condemns him, the doer of them accordingly. . . .'[54]

Conscience is a principle of reflection, according to Butler, in the sense that by means of it we make the intentions, actions, and characters of ourselves and others objects of thought.[55] Butler shared the view of other intuitionists that the moral properties which conscience discerns are logically distinct from all others. 'Everything is what it is, and not another thing. The goodness or badness of actions does not arise from hence, that the epithet, interested or disinterested, may be applied to them, any more than that any other . . . epithet . . . may or not . . . but from their being what they are. . . .'[56] Butler also believed conscience capable of what Hutcheson called 'election', i.e. motivation or excitement to action; he spoke of its 'strength' or 'influence', compared with other forms of motivation, and of its 'restraining' men from evil and 'leading' them to do good.[57]

He conceived of human nature as a system, economy, or constitution. In describing it, he said, regard must be paid, not only to its parts, but to the relations in which they stand, the latter being determined by the use or end for which man exists. The elements of human nature are: (i) A number of *particular passions*, appetites or affections. Each is a direct simple tendency or movement towards a particular external object, or objects, without distinction of means by which they are to be obtained. Hunger, sexual desire, and the desire for esteem are examples. All tend to promote both public and private good, though some more immediately the one than the other. (ii) Two general principles, *benevolence and self-love*, from which actions proceed. These are distinct from the passions, but they may guide effort to gratify the latter. Self-love, for example, 'may put us upon making use of the *proper methods of obtaining*' the pleasure of gratified hunger, but the feeling itself is 'no more self-love than . . . anything in the world'. Benevolence, of course, tends most directly to public, self-love to private, good; yet the two principles are so 'perfectly coincident' that benevolence is a necessary condition of the fullest self-satisfaction and self-love is the chief security of our right behaviour towards society. (iii) *Conscience.* Butler thought that 'it cannot possibly be denied' that there is this principle of reflection in human nature. Any man who did two actions, one helping an innocent person in distress, the other harming a friend with no justification whatever, and then coolly reflected upon them, would inevitably approve of the former and disapprove of the latter. To deny that he would is 'too glaring a falsity to need being confuted'. We shall return to the subject of the authority of conscience, but if the latter is, as Butler affirmed, a faculty 'in kind and in nature supreme over all others, and which bears its own authority of being so', then the end of, and the correct relationship between the elements within, human nature, referred to at the beginning of this paragraph, are self-evident. The end is virtue. The correct relationship is that which conscience prescribes.[58]

30

What precisely does conscience, according to Butler, intuit? His concept of moral fitness was not so much that virtue is appropriate, and vice inappropriate, to the nature of things, as that they are appropriate and inappropriate respectively to the true, or ideal, nature of man. With the Stoics in mind, he said that he had no doubt that this was what ancient moralists really meant when they spoke of living according to nature. And he went on: 'They had a perception that injustice was contrary to their nature, and that pain was so also. They observed these two perceptions totally different, not in degree, but in kind; and the reflecting upon each of them, as they thus stood in their nature, wrought a full intuitive conviction, that more was due and of right belonged to one of these inward perceptions, than to the other; that it demanded in all cases to govern such a creature as man.'[59]

It will be seen from the latter part of this quotation that Butler conceived there to be two aspects to conscience's intuition: (i) the intuition of the *sui generis* unfitness of, for instance, inflicting pain upon the innocent as distinct from the unfitness of pain as such; and (ii) the intuition that perceptions of moral fitness or unfitness ought to direct all man's conscious activity. He compared conscience in these two respects with speculative reason. '. . . it [sc. the moral faculty] determines them [sc. actions] to be good or evil; and also . . . determines itself to be the guide of action and of life, in contradistinction from all other faculties, or natural principles of action: in the very same manner as speculative reason *directly* and naturally judges of speculative truth and falsehood; and at the same time is attended with a consciousness upon *reflection*, that the natural right to judge of them belongs to it.'[60] Conscience, then, discerns moral qualities, in accordance with which it approves or disapproves, and excites to action; while, at the same time, perceiving its own right to do so. It is self-authenticating: 'insomuch that you cannot form a notion of this faculty, conscience, without taking in judgment, direction, superintendency. This is a constituent part of the idea, that is, of the faculty itself: and to preside and govern from the very economy and constitution of man, belongs to it. Had it strength, as it had right: had it power, as it had manifest authority; it would absolutely govern the world.'[61]

Butler faced the question: Why ought we to attend to and follow conscience? He appears to have had two ways of dealing with it. The first is illustrated in the quotation at the end of the last paragraph. In the statement, 'you cannot form a notion of this faculty, conscience, without taking in judgment, direction, superintendency', the 'cannot' is presumably logical, the point being that conscience is by definition a faculty which ought to govern. Then, indeed, 'Ought conscience to govern?' is self-answering. It is logically impossible to doubt that it should. If this was Butler's point is it perfectly sound, but of course merely verbal.

The second way of dealing with the question is illustrated in his words: 'Your obligation to obey this law, is its being the law of your nature . . . it . . . carries its own authority with it, that it is our natural guide; the guide assigned us by the Author of our nature. . . .' As we have seen, he thought it beyond doubt that all men experience the *sui generis* promptings of conscience and that this experience differentiates them from brutes. He did not, of course, deny that conscience may need to be developed or enlightened, and that it can be perverted, but he thought that the experience of its promptings was definitive of man. He argued further that men can as little doubt that the promptings of conscience are given to guide their actions as that their eyes are given to guide their steps.[62]

But supposing these things to be beyond doubt, what follows? If men, as such, experience the promptings of conscience, then it is self-contradictory to say that X is a man, where X does not experience them. Again, if these promptings are experienced as directives to action, then it is self-contradictory to say that Y is one of them, where Y is not so experienced. But in neither case does it necessarily follow that conscience *ought* to be obeyed. There is no logical impossibility in the view that, even though men as such experience the promptings of conscience, they would be better off without them, and, if possible, should be psychologically conditioned to feel them no longer. If the 'should' here is moral, no matter! Assuming the means to be apparent, a man, or group of men, could (logically) make one last moral judgment to the effect that they ought to destroy conscience in themselves and others. Again, there is no logical impossibility in the view that, though the promptings of conscience are experienced as directives to action, they were implanted in us by a malevolent being, and from them we need, if possible, to be saved.

VII. THE DEBATE

The debate between rational intuitionists and 'moral sense' philosophers continued throughout the eighteenth century. To gain some impression of the complicated course which it took, we will extract one or two of the arguments which Hutcheson put up against the rationalists, and note the counter-arguments which are to be found in Balguy and Price.

If reason is the moral faculty, then virtuous action must be reasonable, vicious unreasonable. Reason Hutcheson defined as 'our power of finding out true propositions'; reasonableness, as 'conformity to true propositions, or to truth'. Starting from these definitions, in *Illustrations Upon the Moral Sense*, he set himself to show that schemes which take virtue to consist in conformity to reason, absolute fitness, or agreeableness to the nature of things, and vice in their opposites, presuppose the moral sense.[63]

What do men mean when they speak of reasonableness in action? asked Hutcheson. Have they in mind the motive which causes us to act or the quality which elicits our approval of the act? It seems that they may mean either, for they speak of exciting and justifying reasons. Hutcheson contended that what men say of the former presupposes instincts or affections; of the latter, a moral sense. He found no difficulty in conceiving of exciting reasons. Following Aristotle he differentiated ends as ultimate and subordinate, the latter being means to the former. He was, of course, wedded to the view that the truths which reason finds out are truths about the means of obtaining ends. He said that in every rational action some end is desired or intended; and reason can influence action by discovering truths of the form: 'End $E1$, if achieved, will be a means to end $E2$.' But such a discovery excites us to action, only if we desire $E2$. In this sense, and with this proviso, it makes sense to talk of exciting reasons. But Hutcheson found the notion of a justifying *reason* unintelligible.

Any attempt to define virtue, i.e. action which we are morally *justified* in performing, as *reasonable* action seemed to him to eliminate the distinction between moral good and evil. He made this point in slightly different ways according to what he was taking reasoning to be at the time, but it was always the core of his argument. Here he argued that finding out by reason a true proposition to the effect that a certain action is an efficient means of attaining a certain end does not justify the action, because we may also find out that the worst actions are conducive to their ends and so reasonable in this sense. 'The justifying reasons . . . must be about the ends themselves, especially the ultimate ends. The question then is, "Does conformity to any truth (i.e. reasonableness) make us approve an ultimate end, previously to any moral sense?" For example, we approve pursuing the public good. For what reason? Or what is the truth for conformity to which we call it a reasonable end? I fancy we can find none in these cases, more than we could give for our liking any pleasant fruit.'[64]

Balguy and Price, in opposition to this, believed that it is as definitive of a rational being that he approves of virtue as that he assents to truth. On their view, it makes sense to talk of *both* exciting *and* justifying *reasons*. Approbation of virtue, where other impulses do not interfere, excites a rational being to virtuous action. But what justifies the approbation? 'I answer in one word,' wrote Balguy, 'Necessity. The same necessity which compels men to assent to what is true, forces them to approve what is right and fit.' Virtue, that is to say, has for a rational being the kind of ultimacy which reason itself has. Hutcheson agreed with Balguy that virtue has 'self-worth', that we approve of it for its own sake; but he took it for granted that, if so, the faculty which approves must be a sense. Balguy drew the opposite conclusion. He argued that all the approbation of the moral sense could amount to would be that a given action seems morally good to us at the time. It might not seem so to others, or to us at another time. We would not be justified in approving of it until we knew whether it was morally good *in itself*, because until we did know that, we could not (logically) approve of it as an *ultimate* end.

'Ultimate ends determine themselves as being necessarily approved.' This does not mean, of course, that in practice we always approve of, or aim at, them. Human nature being only partially rational, it does not follow that, if we have an ultimate reason for doing an action, or even if we experience an affection inducing us to do it, we inevitably shall do it. The necessity of which Balguy spoke is essential, not psychological, though he might not have drawn this distinction as we do. His point was that our approbation of ultimate ends must arise from the nature of the ends themselves. This 'must' is logical. It is reason which apprehends the nature, or essence, of things. It is therefore only in so far as man is rational that he can discern and approve of ultimate ends.[65]

Hutcheson next turned to Clarke's view that from the relations in which persons stand to one another there necessarily arises a fitness or unfitness of certain circumstances to certain persons; and morally good actions are agreeable to these relations, morally evil actions are not. Taking as the definition of this fitness 'an agreement of an affection, desire, action, or end to the relations of agents', Hutcheson asked how this agreement might be conceived. (i) Is it equality in dimension: that the affection, etc., has the same bulk and figure as the relation? (ii) Is it the agreement of a corollary to a theorem: when the relation is a true proposition so is the affection, etc.? (iii) Is it preservation: that the affection, etc., tend to preserve the relation as meat does the body? As if God would no longer be our creator or benefactor if we disobeyed him! (iv) Is it pleasantness: that the affection, etc., raise pleasant perceptions in the relation? Though he conceded that this list of conceivable meanings of 'agreement' might not be exhaustive, he was satisfied that he had reduced to absurdity the view that morality consists in relations of agreement or disagreement. Hutcheson subscribed to the Lockeian view that all ideas of relation are complex. He believed that his argument had shown that moral fitness, not being a relation, i.e. a complex idea, must be a simple idea. If simple, again on Lockeian presuppositions, this idea must be given by sense. He concluded: '. . . we must recur upon this scheme [sc. Clarke's] too to a moral sense.' As we have seen, against this Price argued that ideas of relation, whether moral ones like rightness or mathematical ones like equality, are indeed simple ideas, but their source is the understanding or reason.

Hutcheson also subscribed to the Lockeian view that 'relations are not real qualities inherent in external natures'. In attempting to show that moral distinctions are not reducible to relations, he was, in effect, defending their objectivity. It would be a mistake to represent the issue between him and his opponents as simply subjectivism *versus* objectivism. It is important not to confuse Hutcheson's view with what is now called emotivism or prescriptivism. True, Price accused him of reducing morality to 'certain effects in us', and within the terms of the debate this was fair enough. Hutcheson did compare moral properties to Locke's secondary, rather than primary, qualities: that is, to colour, taste, smell etc., rather than to extension, figure or motion. He wrote, for instance, of moral approbation that it 'cannot be supposed an image of anything external, more than the pleasures of harmony, of taste, of smell'. Just as the secondary qualities of colour would not, on the Lockeian view, exist apart from the minds by which they are perceived, no more, on Hutcheson's view, would the moral properties of actions or states of affairs exist apart from the minds which approve or disapprove of them. But Hutcheson is careful to reject two mistaken implications of his view. It does not follow that any man's moral judgment is as good as another's; we may have to correct our moral perceptions by comparing them with those of 'others in good health'. Nor does it follow that moral distinctions depend solely upon the constitution of our minds which could conceivably have been other than it is; there is 'something . . . analogous to our moral sense' in God which guarantees the objectivity of these distinctions.

The point at issue between Hutcheson and the rationalists was whether moral ideas are derived from sense or reason. Notice that, in claiming it to be from the former rather than the latter, Hutcheson compared moral properties *in this crucial respect* to primary, as well as secondary, qualities. He wrote: 'We must not . . . conclude that it is any reasoning antecedent to a moral sense, which determines us to approve the study of public good, any more than we can . . . conclude that we perceive extension, figure, colour, taste, antecedently to a sense. All these sensations are often corrected by reasoning, as well as our approbations of actions as good or evil: and yet nobody ever placed the original idea of extension, figure, colour, or taste, in conformity to reason.' And after the remark quoted above: moral approbation 'cannot be supposed an image of anything external, more than the pleasures of harmony, of taste, of smell', Hutcheson adds immediately: 'But let none imagine, that calling the ideas of virtue and vice perceptions of a sense, upon apprehending the actions and affections of another does diminish their *reality*, more than the like assertions concerning all pleasure and pain, happiness and misery.' (Italics mine.)

I do not think he meant simply psychological reality: that it is undeniable that we experience moral approval or disapproval. This remark should be interpreted in the light of his wish not to deny that there is 'a right or wrong state of our moral sense, as there is in our other senses, according as they represent *their objects to be as they really are*, or . . . otherwise' (italics mine). Locke did not deny that there is something objective, viz. a dispositional property of producing sense experience in us, in things which we perceive as sweet or bitter, etc. And Hutcheson is not concerned to deny the objectivity of morals. His purpose is to show that morality has the same epistemological basis as our knowledge of the external world. In the last analysis, it is grounded in simple ideas of sense, not reason.[66]

Hutcheson engaged the rationalists at another point when he turned his attack on William Wollaston (1659–1724). The latter had interpreted the view, which he found in Clarke, that moral evil consists in the 'endeavour . . . to make things be what they are not',[67] as follows. All actions, in effect, say something about the situations in which they are performed. They signify truth or falsehood. If what they say is true, they are fit, but not if it is false.[68] It is important to notice that Wollaston did not claim that no true propositions can be formulated about evil actions; but that if the proposition which an action constitutes is false, then it is evil. Thus he, in fact, escaped one objection which

Hutcheson brought against his point of view. Hutcheson said: '. . . this conformity [sc. to truth] cannot make a difference among actions, or recommend one more than another either to election or approbation, since any man may make as many truths about villainy as about heroism. . . .' He may indeed, but this was not Wollaston's point. Wollaston had in mind, not what may be said *about* the action, but what it *itself* said.

Hutcheson, however, had more penetrating criticisms to hand. He pointed out against Wollaston that actions are not judged morally good or evil apart from intention. And while intention to deceive sometimes makes an act vicious, and intention to convey true information may make it virtuous, these are by no means always what make acts morally fit or unfit. Again, whatever kind of significance an act putatively has, e.g., concerning the sentiments of the agent, etc., whether it signifies truth or falsehood will necessarily depend upon the capacity of observers to perceive its significance; and to make the virtue or vice of action dependent upon the perspicacity of observers is patently ridiculous.

It is difficult to be certain just what Wollaston meant by signifying truth or falsehood. Hutcheson considered the possibility that he meant that a good action is one from which true propositions can be drawn by just reasoning. But if the premiss that an act exists is true, then only true conclusions can be deduced by just reasoning, whether the act is good or evil. Are good actions then such that a just reasoner would infer from them that the opinions of the agent, concerning what to do, given his ends and his circumstances, are true? Hutcheson showed why not. Suppose a constitution of nature C, an end of the agent E, and an act A, performed by this agent in these circumstances. Could we infer from A alone that the agent's opinions about what to do, given E and C, are true? Even if we knew the truth about C, A's not fulfilling what we take to be E could not, in itself, prove that the agent's opinions were false. We might simply have been mistaken about E. And if C and E were evil, then obviously the agent's opinion might be true, yet the act A be evil.

Hutcheson commented on Wollaston's remark: 'signifying falsehood is altering the natures of things, and making them to be

39

what they are not, or desiring at least to make them be what they are not.' He could not make sense of this. Even the worst actions *cannot* alter the nature of things. And if by the nature of things one means the laws of nature, then the worst actions need not involve any *desire* to change them. The murderer, for instance, does not, as such, wish the laws of nature to be other than they are. True, he changes things — he makes his living victim dead — but if changing, or desiring to change, things makes action evil, then, as Hutcheson pointed out, every artificer, purchaser, magistrate, etc., will be guilty of evil-doing.

Hutcheson made a point which was later taken up by Hume[69] and others. Wollaston's view leaves unanswered the inescapable question: why is what signifies truth said to be morally good and what does not morally evil? 'Should he not first have shown what was moral evil; and that every lie was such?'

Hutcheson also discovered a quite distinct idea of moral good and evil implicit in Wollaston's view. The latter conceded that there is little evil in some actions, e.g. throwing away what has small use or value, and great evil in others, e.g. being ungrateful to God. But the one is just as much a denial of truth as the other! So, in Wollaston's opinion, said Hutcheson, 'virtue and vice increase, as the importance of propositions affirmed or denied; therefore virtue and vice are not the same with signification of truth or falsehood'.

Balguy and Price did not attempt to defend Wollaston against such criticism. Price did suggest that Wollaston might have meant no more than that a man who, for instance, neglects the worship of God thereby asserts, figuratively speaking, that he is self-originating and self-sufficient; but he was alive to the point that, if we say that a truth is denied in such a case, it is not only the truth that God exists, but also that man ought to worship Him. 'How plain is it here that the very thing that gives ground for the application of this language in this instance, is our perceiving, antecedently to this application that such a manner of acting in such circumstances, is wrong? The same is true in all other instances; nor, independently of this perception, could we ever know when to say, that an action affirms or denies truth.' Balguy and Price would have had no quarrel with Wollaston, if he had said simply that some of the true propositions which reason finds out express necessary truths about morality. But it does not follow from this, as Wollaston seems to have thought, that the concept of right can be reduced to that of truth. The fitness of right actions to situations, with which morality is concerned, is, like the fitness of true propositions to facts, a perception of reason. But the two kinds of fitness are logically distinct.[70]

VIII. WHAT CONSTITUTES VIRTUE?

Both 'moral sense' philosophers and rational intuitionists conceived action to be virtuous only when the agent is aware of it as such and chooses to perform it freely. The moral faculty, whether sense or reason, is reflexive; and it must be operative wherever there is virtue or vice. Shaftesbury said: 'if he [sc. the agent] cannot reflect on what he himself does . . . so as to take notice of what is worthy or honest . . . he has not the character of being virtuous.'[71] Price said that 'liberty' and 'intelligence' are essentials of practical virtue.[72] It is characteristic, then, of virtuous action to be approved by the moral faculty of the agent and freely chosen by his will. But what are the characteristics which engage this approbation and move to this choice?

The 'moral sense' philosophers held that a virtuous act is one which proceeds from a benevolent 'affection', i.e. motive or intention. There are, however, slight differences in the account of this affection which Shaftesbury and Hutcheson gave. The former appears to have thought that it must be an affection which, in normal circumstances, gives rise to the good of the social whole to which the agent belongs: 'if . . . the subject of the affection (be) such as may with advantage to society be ever in the same manner prosecuted, or affected; this must necessarily constitute what we call equity and right in any action'.[73] But it was enough for Hutcheson if the affection was benevolent. There has, however, been some discussion as to whether he held this view, that virtue consists in the intention or motive, consistently. He wrote: 'In comparing the moral qualities of actions . . . we are led by our moral sense . . . to judge thus: that in equal degrees of happiness, expected to proceed from the action, the virtue is in proportion to the number of persons to whom the happiness shall extend . . . and in equal numbers the virtue is as the quantity of the happiness . . . so that, that action is best, which procures the greatest happiness for the greatest numbers. . . .'[74] This certainly sounds like Utilitarianism, and some readers think that Hutcheson turned from the view that the morality of actions is to be judged from their *motives or intentions* to the view that it is to be judged from their social *effects*. But others dispute this. They point out that Hutcheson spoke here of the 'expected', not the actual, effects of action, and infer that it was still the quality of the affection which was in his mind. They contend that Hutcheson regarded the number whose happiness an agent intends to produce, or the quantity of happiness which he seeks to create, as indices of the purity of his benevolent affection.[75]

Butler also held that the morality of an action is to be judged by its motive or intention. 'Intention of such and such consequences, indeed, is always included; for it is part of the action itself: but though the intended good or bad consequences do not follow, we have exactly the same sense of the action as if they did.'[76] Butler did not, however, think that the only virtuous affection is benevolence, i.e. intention to produce the well-being of others. If two men are competing for the same object, he said, equal well-being might be achieved by a third party helping *either* to secure it. But if one of the competitors is the third party's friend or benefactor, and the other is not, would not this third party have a duty to help him rather than the other? Again, the same effect in terms of well-being might be achieved by taking a man's money forcibly from him and giving it to another, whose pleasure counterbalances the misery of the rightful owner, but would such an action be right? Butler concluded, from such instances, that friendship, gratitude, deceit, violence, injustice, and such motives, determine morality as well as benevolence. The latter may be the whole of virtue in God, but it is not so in us.[77]

For all this talk of benevolence, however, there are indications in Shaftesbury and Butler of what may be called basic Hobbism. Shaftesbury distinguished two questions from one another: 'What is virtue?' and 'What constitutes our obligation to virtue?' This is surely a distinction without a difference; for virtue is, by definition, obligatory, and the answer to the first question also answers the second. However, Shaftesbury did distinguish them, and his answer to the second was the putative fact that 'to be well affected towards the public interest and one's own, is not only consistent, but inseparable'. This can only mean that we ought to seek the public good because it is essential to our own. Butler is even more explicit. 'Let it be allowed, though virtue or moral rectitude does indeed consist in affection to and pursuit of what is right and good, as such; yet, that when we sit down in a cool hour, we can neither justify to ourselves this or any other pursuit, till we are convinced that it will be for our happiness, or at least not contrary to it.' If we take 'can justify' in a fully moral sense, the conclusion is inescapable that this means that what constitutes virtue is in the last analysis self-interest. Hutcheson and Price were at some pains to dissociate themselves from such opinions.[78]

The rational intuitionists, like Butler, rejected the view that benevolence is the whole of virtue. There are, in Cudworth's words, other things 'which the intellectual nature, obligeth to of itself'.[79] Later rationalists have called benevolence and these other things *prima facie* obligations. In so far as any action is the fulfilling of one or more such *prima facie* duties, it is obligatory. Cudworth gave, as examples, 'to keep faith and perform covenants' and 'to obey God'. He was not very concerned, however, to list these obligations, but simply to insist that they subsist by nature not by will. They are obligatory, not because any one, even God, wills them, but 'in themselves'.

Clarke and Price did attempt more comprehensive lists. The former said that there are three 'rules of righteousness' from which 'all the other and smaller instances of duty do naturally flow, or may without difficulty be derived'. They are as follows: (i) *Duty to God*, which consists in worshipping Him and doing what we believe Him to will; (ii) *Duty to others*, which has two aspects, equity and love (or universal benevolence); and (iii) *Duty to self*.

The first aspect of duty to others is defined: 'that . . . we so deal with every man, as in like circumstances we could reasonably expect he should deal with us.' The reason which forbids inequitable conduct, Clarke argued, is 'the very same' as that which 'forces' one to affirm that 'if one line or number be equal to another, that other is reciprocally equal to it'. That is to say, to treat a man differently from the way in which we think that he ought, in similar circumstances, to treat us is self-contradictory. Now, we could certainly accuse of inconsistency anyone who said that act A was obligatory in situation X because the latter has such and such characteristics, but not in situation Y which also has these characteristics. To defend himself, the speaker would have to show that, in some morally relevant respect, Y differed from X. But the reason why what we *say* must not be self-contradictory cannot be applied, as Clarke wished to apply it, to what we *do*. Self-contradiction evacuates a statement of cognitive meaning. But if we object to men acting in ways which do not conform to their moral principles, the reason is not — except in a figure of speech — that their actions do not make sense. Acts are not statements. The reason for our objection is a principle of conduct — that men ought to practice what they preach.

The other aspect of duty to others is love or universal benevolence. Clarke seems to say two things here, one logical, one empirical. If it is reasonable to seek the good of others, then it is most reasonable to seek this to the fullest extent, and a being who is completely fulfilling his duty will 'do all the good he can to all his fellow-men'. Given Clarke's presupposition — that to do one's duty is to be reasonable — the argument is valid. The other thing Clarke says, however, is less defensible. Since men 'cannot live comfortably in independent families . . . they *naturally* desire to increase their dependencies . . . and this . . . terminates in . . . the community of mankind'. This may or may not be true, but either way it is simply a fact about human nature. Clarke goes on: man is '*consequently* obliged, as the necessary and only effectual means to that end [sc. the community of mankind] to embrace them all with universal love and benevolence' (italics mine in both quotations). I think there is some confusion in Clarke's mind at this point between two senses of 'nature'. The nature of man may mean either what man *is*, or — as some Greek philosophers used the expression — what man is ideally, i.e. what he *ought* to be. The two senses are quite distinct. But Clarke seems to think here that because it is a fact (if it is) that men *are* gregarious (their nature — first sense), it follows that they *ought* (their nature — second sense) to be universally benevolent. But, of course, this is a deduction of 'ought' from 'is', and falls under the objections which we have listed above.

Duty to self is the duty of each man to preserve his life and develop his talents to the full. As Clarke presents it, this duty is parasitic upon the other two. A man should fulfil it 'as may best fit and enable him to perform his duty in all other instances'; and because 'He that sent us into the world . . . and . . . appointed us our station here . . . has alone authority to dismiss and discharge us'.[80]

Price listed six 'heads of virtue', as he called them.[81] He did not claim completeness for his list; but he did claim that 'all men at all times have agreed' that those which he lists are self-evidently obligations. On his lips the claim that all reasonable beings intuit these heads of virtue is analytic, for not to do so is to be a 'rebel against reason'. But he did think, at the same time, that an empirical investigation would show that, apart from cases which can be explained as due to mistakes of fact, differences of circumstance, and prevalence of corrupting custom or education, all men, whatever their age or society, have, in fact, intuited these heads of virtue. We shall return to this point below, but first let us look at Price's list.

(i) *Duty to God* is the 'whole of that regard, subjection and homage we owe him'. This duty is derivative from two others. It binds us because God is our 'creator, governor, and benefactor', that is to say, it is a particular instance of our duties (*a*) to obey our superiors ('creator, governor'), and (*b*) to be grateful to our benefactors ('benefactor'). If they are prepared to concede that there are self-evident duties at all, I think Price's modern readers will be more inclined to regard (*b*) as such than (*a*).

(ii) *Duty to self*, said Price, constitutes incontestable proof that benevolence is not the whole of virtue. He wrote: 'If it is my duty to promote the good of another and to abstain from hurting him; the same must most certainly be my duty with regard to myself. It would be contrary to all reason to deny this.' It seems plausible to argue that if X is intrinsically good, then it is good whether it is my good or someone else's. In the case of virtue and knowledge, for instance, most men would probably agree that these are good and we have a duty to maximise them for ourselves as well as for others. But the case is different if we think of happiness as a good. Is it intrinsically good, as knowledge and virtue are? Most men would probably agree that the happiness of *others* is a good which we ought to seek as we seek virtue or knowledge. But would they say that one ought to maximise one's *own* happiness with the same application? Probably not. Here Price failed to see that it is not contrary to all reason to seek a good for others and not for ourselves, since its being theirs, not ours, may be what makes it good.[82]

(iii) *Beneficence*, i.e. duty to promote the public good, is, said Price, 'the most general and leading consideration in all our enquiries concerning *right*'. Where the public good in question is 'very considerable', this duty outweighs any other.

(iv) *Gratitude* to a benefactor, said Price, is 'but one out of a great variety of instances wherein particular facts and circumstances constitute a fitness of a different behaviour to different persons'. His examples are, to fellow-countrymen, members of one's profession or club, or one's family and friends.

I think most readers will agree with Price that we have obligations of beneficence and gratitude (and the others to which he refers under 'gratitude'). But his contention that, where public interest is very considerable, beneficence cancels every other obligation is not indisputable. It is of very great public concern that murderers should be caught, but if one of our children or friends, having committed murder, asked our assistance, should we think it our duty to hand him over to the police? If we thought him insane, we might hand him over readily enough. But in that case would it be the public good, or his own, which we had in mind?

(v) *Veracity*. 'Truth then', wrote Price, 'necessarily recommends itself to our preference. And the essence of *lying* consisting in using established signs in order to *deceive*, it must be disapproved by all beings upon the same ground with those on which truth and knowledge are desired by them, and right judgment

47

preferred to mistake and ignorance.' The argument is as follows. A lie aims to persuade someone that what is is not, or vice versa. Reason, the power which apprehends what is, rejects this contradiction. But reason is not only the cognitive, but also the moral, faculty and it therefore rejects the lie in moral judgment just as in cognition, all 'consequences apart'. Well, does it? I think many men would judge that if a lie was to have no consequences whatever — in this world or any other — then to tell it is morally indifferent. More cogent objections arise when Price goes on to say that promise-keeping is simply 'a branch or instance of veracity'. To break a promise is to lie 'as really as if he [the promiser] had declared what he knew to be false past or present fact'. The only difference, said Price, is that a lie refers to the past or present, a promise to the future. But, against this, let us suppose a reasonable and morally responsible man to be in three situations. First: he promises A to do X, but then A tells him that he does not want him to do X. He now feels no compunction in not doing it. But the difference between promising and simply lying comes out if we ask: would he, in other contexts, tell a lie with an easy conscience simply because someone said that he would not mind him doing so (there being no question of loyalty as a friend, etc.)? Second: our man resolves to give himself an outing. If he breaks this resolve, he has in some sense broken a promise to himself. But will he feel guilty about that as he would if he had broken a promise to take his child out? Third: suppose it is war-time, and our man is caught by the enemy. He lies when questioned about where he was the night before and feels no compunction in doing so. But, as an honourable man, would he have felt none if he had told this lie to a friend or to his wife?

These three cases bring out two points: (a) From the first two it appears that an obligation to keep promises is not experienced as an obligation to be loyal to the truth as such, but to persons within specific relationships. This obligation arises only where some other person is involved and it is terminable at will by this other person. (b) From the third case it appears that, so far from the obligation to keep promises being a special instance of the obligation to tell the truth, the reverse is the case. Underlying the duty of veracity, it would appear, there is an agreement or 'passive' understanding between persons that the truth will be told.[83] This contractual obligation is non-existent between enemies, but different degrees of it are implicit in citizenship, friendship, marriage, etc.

(vi) *Justice*. Price confines himself almost exclusively to that part of justice which concerns property. Like Locke and Paine, he believed that the right to property is as original and inalienable as that to life or liberty. His modern readers are unlikely to agree. It is significant that in the *Universal Declaration of Human Rights*, proclaimed by the General Assembly of the United Nations in 1948, Article III reads: 'Everyone has a right to life, liberty and security of person', but it is not until Article XVII that we read: 'Everyone has a right to his own property alone as well as in association with others. No one shall be arbitrarily deprived of his property.' Note this last sentence! It leaves wide scope for different interpretations of 'arbitrarily'. Price did recognise the justice of treating persons in accordance with their merits. But even this he limited by the rights of property. Doubtless Price would have agreed that it is right to take a man's property, or some of it, away, if he does wrong; but he expressly repudiates the idea that being a worthier person is a ground for giving one man any other man's property.

It is a little surprising that Price says nothing about the justice of treating men in accordance with their needs. This is perhaps a more common conception of justice in the twentieth century than it was in the eighteenth; nevertheless, in Price's day, good men surely recognised an obligation to help the needy! Yet neither under beneficence nor justice does Price refer specifically to the claim which the weak have upon the strong.

Price was firmly set against any utilitarian account of justice, and this claim would have been a better argument against it than the one which he used, namely, that justice recognises merit, not simply social good. It may be plausibly argued, against Price here, that the public good is served by rewarding good men and punishing wicked, and so the ultimate justification of recognising merit is utilitarian. But the duty to help unfortunates (e.g. by medical care, pensions, training schemes, etc.), cannot be given such a utilitarian justification. This duty, most men would feel, requires more of them than what is strictly necessary to reduce the burden on society which the unfortunates constitute. By purely utilitarian criteria it might well seem advisable to spend far less time and money on the handicapped than we do; but I do not think that the ordinary moral consciousness, to which Price makes appeal, would accept this as right, even so.

IX. SOME OUTSTANDING QUESTIONS

(i) HOW DOES ONE DECIDE BETWEEN CONFLICTING OBLIGATIONS?

A number of *prima facie* obligations may, of course, be instantiated in a given situation. These may, as Price said, 'interfere'. Duty to self, for instance, may conflict with beneficence; and either or both with gratitude, veracity, or justice.[84] Does this mean that a moral principle such as 'One ought to preserve one's life' is self-evident, yet there are cases where one ought not to preserve one's life? Price apparently thought so, but he refused to admit that this destroys the analogy which he had drawn between moral principles and mathematical axioms. He pointed out that it is often as difficult to solve a mathematical, as a moral, problem. True; but the real point is that, if there are exceptions to moral principles, the latter are not self-evident in the same sense as mathematical axioms.

Some later intuitionists have tried to eliminate this difference by taking moral principles to refer to 'tendencies' which certain actions have.[85] On this view, moral principles have the form, for instance, 'All acts of promise-keeping have a tendency to be obligatory.' Such a principle is self-evident, it is said, and there are no exceptions to it. So it is comparable to universal, self-evident, mathematical axioms, such as: 'Things equal to the same thing are equal to one another.' But the objection to this talk of 'tendencies' is, as Mr. P. F. Strawson has pointed out, that to say, 'All acts of promise-keeping have a tendency to be obligatory' is simply to say that most, but not all, of the class of actions which fulfil promises are obligatory.[86] The breakdown of the analogy between mathematical axioms and moral principles would not matter if the analogy were simply a useful working comparison. But intuitionists such as Price wish to argue that moral principles are self-evident *just as* mathematical axioms are, and *therefore* the former, like the latter, constitute an intuition of the nature of things. Against that view the breakdown of the analogy is damning.

Where obligations conflict, Price said, they must be 'weighed' against each other.[87] But we cannot weigh without scales. What is the scale of measurement here? The situation Price refers to is common enough. In most cases where a moral decision has to be made, it is not simply a matter of seeing how one principle applies in that case, but which of a number of principles is to take precedence. In such situations, how is one to decide what one ought to do? The answer which intuitionists give is apparently that one 'feels' or 'sees' what one ought to do. This is plainly intended to mean something more than simply that one decides what to do. But can we make it mean more? The given situation may be familiar or novel. If familiar, then it may make sense to say that the instantiated principles come to us with certain 'weights', if by that we mean that they come to us graded in accordance with past decisions which we have made in similar situations. But then all that this talk of 'weight' amounts to is that, in the past, we have decided to act in one way rather than another. If the situation is novel, when does one know which obligation 'feels' heavier? Surely, when one has decided what one ought to do! As J-P. Sartre wrote of this 'feeling', in discussing the pupil who asked whether he ought to stay with his mother or join the Free French in England, 'feeling is formed by the deeds that one does; therefore I cannot consult it as a guide to action'.[88] To the question 'How am I to decide which of conflicting obligations to fulfil?' the answer 'By weighing them against each other' is really no answer. All it comes to is the triviality, 'Decide by deciding'!

(ii) DO ALL MEN INTUIT THE 'HEADS' OF VIRTUE?

The differences in the moral codes to which men hold, or have held, are multifarious. Those opposed to intuitionism have made great play with this fact. Bertrand Russell,[89] for instance, thinks it significant that among head-hunters in Borneo a man could not marry until he brought a dowry of a certain number of heads, whereas in our society we should not regard it as our duty, as parents, to make sure that a man was a murderer before we allowed him to marry our daughter. How, then, can it be affirmed that all men intuit the same *prima facie* obligations? The intuitionists' reply is that, in our society, we should regard it as a parent's duty to have some evidence that a suitor could take care of his daughter before consenting to marriage. It is purely circumstantial that in Borneo murder constitutes such evidence, but not in Britain. With such allowances for circumstances altering cases, it is claimed, all men do intuit certain obligations, either as universal principles or as particular duties which recur in certain situations.

Price suggested some further causes of the differences in moral codes. Custom, education, or example may 'alter the direction' of our moral ideas and connect them with the wrong objects. Instinctive determinations, such as parental love, may distort our sense of duty. The 'interference' of moral principles with one another may confuse our judgment. In support of his view that beneath such superficial causes of difference there is unanimity, Price contended that, when men judge others, or rationalise their own conduct, they always betray an acknowledgment of one or more of his heads of virtue.[90]

It must be admitted that, when these points are taken into account, there has been remarkable agreement in different ages and societies, at least concerning certain broad moral principles. Perhaps some recognition of the claims which Price classified under 'gratitude' or 'veracity' is essential to the very existence of society, and that is why these obligations have apparently been universally recognised in some form or other. Of course, they are restricted to the society in question and this is sometimes very small. Only with the emergence of the idea of the universal society of mankind are obligations given universal application. None the less, the intuitionists' basic empirical claim that there are certain duties, which the majority of men in all ages or cultures have recognised, is perhaps stronger than many critics have admitted.

(iii) IS IT OUR DUTY TO DO WHAT IS RIGHT OR WHAT WE THINK RIGHT?

We have seen that the intuitionists believed action virtuous only when the agent was aware of it as such. There are issues here which Price seems to have been the first to bring out clearly,[91] though he himself seems to have thought that Hutcheson to some extent had anticipated him. Hutcheson wrote: 'An act is materially good when in fact it tends to the interest of the system . . . whatever were the affections of the agent. . . . An action is formally good when it flowed from a good affection.'[92] This distinction, Price said, is 'not entirely different' from his between abstract, or absolute, and practical virtue. But actually the contrast in Hutcheson's mind was really between the effects and the motives of action and this is a quite distinct issue from absolute and practical virtue. 'Abstract' or 'absolute' virtue is what an agent in the given circumstances *really* ought to do; 'practical' or 'relative' virtue is what the agent *thinks* he ought to do. The former had, for Price, in a metaphysical sense, 'real existence'. He argued that the very concept of practical virtue implies absolute: for there must logically be a distinction between what is the case, and what is thought to be the case, if the concept of practical virtue is to be intelligible. Certainly we draw a distinction, in ordinary speech, between what we think virtue to be and what it really is. For instance, we say 'I thought, at the time, that I was doing my duty, but I see now that I wasn't.' But this is adequately accounted for as a contrast between what I thought *then*, and what I think *now*, and does not require a metaphysical entity, the absolutely virtuous act, for its explanation.

Price rejects the view that it is our duty to do the absolutely virtuous action because to know what the latter is in any situation we should need to know the 'capacities' and 'relations' of the agent and the 'consequences' of his actions in full, and this much we never can know unerringly. He is surely correct. In order to know that X is an absolutely virtuous act I should have to know (*a*) that in the situation there is a thing of the kind T, capable of having a state of the kind S effected in it, and (*b*) that the situation is such that my act X will cause T to assume a state of the kind S. But I may not know (*a*); for instance, I may not know that in a given situation there is someone in need whose need I could relieve. And as for (*b*), while I may believe it to be the case, I can *never* know with absolute certainty that it is. I can never know that an act of mine will accomplish what I intend that it shall. Since we never know what the absolutely virtuous action is, the following absurd consequences would follow, as H. A. Prichard and W. D. Ross pointed out,[93] if it were our duty. (i) We could never do our duty because it is our duty, for this must mean because we know it to be our duty. (ii) We may have done our duty on some past occasion when we believed that we were doing what we ought *not* to do. (iii) We may do our duty and *not know* that it is our duty.

So, while not retracting his insistence that the absolutely virtuous act has real existence, Price contended that 'in a different sense' the practically virtuous act has 'real virtue'. It is our duty to do what we think we ought to do. He was careful to point out that he is not saying here that whatever we *think* things to be, that they *are*. The distinction between what is and what is thought to be the case remains. It is the case that an act which it is our duty to do is one which we think we ought to do. If anyone thinks that this is not the case, he is mistaken.

A question arises, however, as to the degree of subjectivity which is here being introduced into the notion of duty. Did Price think that it is our duty to do what is *in fact* obligatory in such circumstances as the agent *thinks* the present ones to be (call this view PV-1), or to do what the agent *thinks* obligatory in such circumstances as he *thinks* the present ones to be (call this view PV-2)? He said that moral agents are 'liable to mistake the circumstances they are in and consequently to form erroneous judgments concerning their own obligations' and this would only require PV-1. But it is clear from what he said about conflicts of obligation that he went further. Price believed that the heads of virtue are certainly known by all reasonable men; but their judgment is fallible when it comes to 'weighing' these against each other in particular situations. He realised that the agent may do his duty even when he is mistaken on either of two levels: (i) as to whether a particular situation provides grounds for a single moral principle; or (ii), where a situation appears to give grounds for more than one principle, as to which of these should cancel the others. The first kind of mistake would be covered by PV-1; but the second requires PV-2.

X. CRITIQUE OF INTUITIONISM

The fundamental belief of all the authors with whom we are concerned in this study was that there are moral truths which, when known, are known by intuition; and, if men do not know them, their defect of intuition is comparable either to a defect of physical sight or of intellectual discernment. We will deal with the elements of this belief in turn.

First, does it make sense to speak of knowing by intuition? The word 'know' usually differs in meaning from 'believe'. To know X is not simply to believe, i.e. to be convinced, or *fee* sure, of X. Admittedly, 'know' is sometimes used with some such meaning. People say that they know when they mean that they feel very sure. But this feeling often turns out to have been mistaken. It is intelligible, then, in any context to insist on a distinction between knowing and feeling sure. 'You say that you know. But do you really *know* or do you only feel sure?'

When 'know' is used in accordance with this distinction between knowing and merely believing firmly, there are three conditions which must be fulfilled. I am entitled to say 'I know X' if: (i) X is true. I cannot know that London is the capital of Scotland. (ii) I believe X. It does not make sense to say 'I know London is the capital of England but I do not believe it.' (iii) I have a satisfactory answer to the question, 'How do you know X?', giving me what Professor A. J. Ayer calls 'the right to be sure'.[94]

Is 'By intuition' such an answer? Three objections can be brought against it. (i) It assimilates the third condition of knowledge to the second; it simply reaffirms that one feels sure. (ii) Intuition is indistinguishable in cases where it is ultimately shown to have been mistaken from those in which it is not. For instance, so-called 'men of destiny', such as Hitler, claim to know intuitively what to do to ensure victory in battle or success in some other enterprise. Sometimes their intuitions, when acted upon, meet with success, sometimes with failure. But, so far as one can tell, there is no discernible difference in the two cases, so far as the feeling of certainty is concerned. (iii) We do not, in fact, accept this answer. If we did, we should persist in our claim to know by intuition, whatever contrary evidence came to light. But only mad men do that. If sufficient weight of evidence comes to light, we are always prepared to concede that what we claimed to know by intuition we did not know.

Now, can failure to intuit such moral 'truths' as that promise-breaking is wrong, be attributed, as intuitionists have often attributed it, to a sort of blindness or stupidity? Take first the analogy with physical blindness. If a group of people, looking at a lawn, all saw a tree on it, except one, Smith, then, given obvious conditions (that no one was obstructing Smith's line of vision, etc.), we should conclude that Smith's sight was in some way defective. Similarly, intuitionists argue, if Smith does not 'see' the wrongness of promise-breaking, we are entitled to say that he is morally 'blind'.

The first and most obvious objection to this view is that there are no *agreed* tests for deciding whether or not a man is morally 'blind', as there are for deciding whether or not his eyesight is defective. It is conceivable that Smith does not see the tree on the lawn because he is deceived by some trick of the light; and it is even possible that there is no tree there and everyone, except Smith, is suffering from an hallucination. If such possibilities worry us, how can we eliminate them? We can take Smith to a specialist who will test his eyes. The tests will be *independent* of Smith's not seeing the tree; and they will be such as other specialists — and plain men in so far as they understand them — consider appropriate for testing eyesight. But there do not seem to be any such independent, agreed tests which all moralists — much less all plain men — accept as tests for moral 'blindness'.

This contention may conceivably be questioned. Suppose Smith does not 'see' that promise-breaking is wrong. We could investigate his other moral beliefs and his conduct. If we found that he rejected other moral principles (besides that concerning promise-breaking), which most other men accept, and that his behaviour was frequently such as most other men would call licentious or dissolute, would not these discoveries constitute agreed, independent, corroborative evidence of his moral 'blindness'? Yes. But the point is that such evidence may *not* exist. Yet, even if Smith is at one with most other men in his moral beliefs and conduct on everything except promise-breaking, the intuitionist, *qua* intuitionist, is committed to explaining his failure to 'see' the wrongness of promise-breaking as due to a defect of intuition. He does not 'see' it because he is morally 'blind'. Presumably the intuitionist means more by this than the vacuous tautology, he does not 'see' it because he does not 'see' it. Yet what more does this tell us than that? Recall the tree on the lawn. To say that Smith does not see it because his eyesight is defective explains why he does not see it because there is more to having defective eyesight than simply not seeing this tree on the lawn. If Smith failed every test for defective eyesight known to specialists, yet still did not see the tree on the lawn, it would tell us nothing to say that he did not see it because his eyesight was defective, which we did not already know when we were told simply that he did not see it. Nor does it tell us anything, when the intuitionist says that Smith does not 'see' the wrongness of promise-breaking because something is wrong with his capacity for moral intuition, where there is no further evidence of moral 'blindness'. All the intuitionist is saying, in such a case, is that Smith does not 'see' it because he does not 'see' it.

Is the comparison with intellectual stupidity any more plausible? If Smith's moral judgment on an act in a particular situation differs from that of other men, then this could be because he lacks the intelligence to see how a certain moral principle, or principles, apply in such situations. His 'stupidity', then, would be comparable to that of a man who could not see how certain axioms, rules of inference, etc., can be used to solve a mathematical problem. But suppose Smith simply says that he cannot 'see' the wrongness of promise-breaking. This is not a matter of unravelling the moral aspects of a complicated situation, but of 'seeing' a single principle which rational intuitionists say that all men who are not morally stupid do 'see'. Can Smith's failure to 'see' it be plausibly called a kind of stupidity? If Smith is a moron, then, of course, he may not understand the sentence, 'Promise-breaking is wrong', but *ex hypothesi* any comparison with such stupidity is excluded. The intuitionist does not say that Smith cannot understand the meaning of this sentence, but that he cannot 'see' the moral truth which it expresses. On the rational intuitionist's own presuppositions, however, does this make sense? He compares principles such as 'Promise-breaking is wrong' with mathematical axioms. Well, would it make sense if someone, who was being instructed in Euclidean geometry, said that he did not see the truth of 'Things equal to the same thing are equal to one another'? This is not a proposition which he is required to judge true or false. It is a definition which, if he is going to do Euclidean geometry at all, he must accept. He may, of course, refuse to accept it. But if this refusal is called stupidity, then to say that anyone refused to accept the axiom because he was stupid would be to utter the tautology that he refused to accept it because he refused to accept it. Similarly, if moral principles are comparable to mathematical axioms, to say that Smith does not think that promise-breaking is wrong because he is stupid is vacuous. All it means is that he does not accept this principle because he does not accept it.

XI. CONCLUSION

The writers whom we have considered in this study were men of their time. They worked out their moral philosophy in the light of contemporary empirical facts and the alternative philosophical viewpoints which then prevailed. But times have changed. New approaches have emerged in philosophy and influenced the account which thinkers give of morals; and it would seem that even the empirical facts of morality are not what they were.

The rationalists and the 'moral sense' philosophers claimed that all men intuit certain moral truths to be self-evident; and that any plain man has only to look into his own breast to become aware of the overriding authority of conscience. Now, unless these empirical claims had, in the past, answered to something in the experience of their readers, the ethical intuitionists would have been quickly forgotten. They, and many of their readers in the past so far as one can tell, did indeed 'hear' the magisterial 'voice' of conscience within; and there was, in point of fact, a high degree of unanimity in its deliverances as between one man and another. The reasons for this state of things are perhaps not far to seek. In times when authority — parental, pedagogic, and priestly — is austere and unquestioned, it is hardly surprising if men develop imperious super-egos. And where the prevailing moral code is clear and stable, it is not surprising to find them at one on where their duty lies. Past ages have, of course, all had their moral rebels. But, by contrast with our own day, the times in which our authors wrote were marked by uncritical respect for authority and general agreement on moral issues. Today consciences appear to be less imperious; and they are certainly less assured and agreed in their pronouncements upon any issue. This contrast, between the empirical facts of man's moral life then and now, explains, in part at least, why ethical intuitionism, which has seemed to many past generations plausible and convincing, strikes a modern reader like Mr. J. O. Urmson as 'obscurantist', and, if we are to believe Professor P. Edwards, seems 'incredible' to most contemporary students of philosophy nowadays, when they first encounter it.[95]

Because so many moral judgments appeared to eighteenth-century intuitionists clear-cut and indisputable, they concluded that the moral properties of actions or states of affairs are objective. They are, that is to say, not matters of variable human opinion, but part of the unchanging structure of reality. What account, then, was to be given of the faculty which discerns them? Turning to philosophical empiricism for the answer, Shaftesbury and Hutcheson said that, since our most reliable guides to the nature of objective reality are the elemental data of our senses, the moral faculty must be a sense. The rationalists contended that the deliverances of the moral faculty are more certain than that view would allow. It is conceivable that our senses should have been other than they are and that the reality which we experience through them should be other than it seems to us to be. So, if moral intuitions are attributed to a sense, it becomes conceivable that they also could have been other than they are, or could mislead us. This the rationalists would not have. They saw that it would have meant conceding, not only that promise-breaking, for instance, might have *seemed to us* to be right, but that it could conceivably have *been* right. This latter, they said, is as inconceivable as that two and two should not make four, or the whole not be greater than one of its parts. To what, then, must we attribute moral intuitions, if not to a sense? Cartesian intuitionism gave them their answer. According to this philosophy, the ultimate logical constituents of reasoning are clear and distinct ideas which cannot conceivably be other than they are. These are apprehended by reason, or understanding, in its intuitive function. Euclidean axioms provide one example of clear and distinct ideas. The rationalists believed that certain fundamental moral intuitions (such as that promise-breaking is wrong) provide another. The givenness, or objectivity, of morals, they held, can only be accounted for adequately, if the moral faculty is taken to be reason.

Both these philosophical viewpoints reify moral judgment in two ways. They conceive of some 'thing', or entity, the moral faculty, existing 'within' the minds of men; and of another kind of 'thing', the moral properties of actions or states of affairs, existing 'out there' in objective reality. Moral judgment occurs when the 'thing' in man 'comes into touch with' the 'thing' in objective reality. Of course, these are 'things' in a qualified, non-spatio-temporal sense. The 'thing' in man is said to be spiritual, not material; and the 'things' in reality to be, not natural, but 'non-natural', properties. But the reification remains. Behind moral words are the entities to which they refer and the entity which uses them so to refer. Moral experience is the activity, or interrelationship, of these entities. Moral philosophy is the study of how they work. Moral language is the medium within which they work, or the tool which they use.

But need we postulate such entities? It has seemed to many modern philosophers that here is a clear case for *Occam's Razor*: Entities must not be multiplied without necessity. If we dispense with these entities, we are left only with the language which men use. But could not an intelligible and satisfactory account of moral judgment be given in terms of this alone?

Suppose we accept the contention of rational intuitionists that moral thinking, like mathematical, can be broken down ulti-mately into appeals to what is axiomatic or self-evident. Then, in making a moral judgment, one is applying a principle, or prin-ciples, to which one is committed, just as in geometry one is applying axioms. The principles referred to are 'self-evident', at least in the sense that one cannot justify them in terms of anything beyond themselves, and perhaps also in the sense that one cannot conceive of any circumstances in which one would be prepared to abandon them. What is going on in moral judgment would now amount to this: words like 'right' and 'good' are being used to commend actions or states of affairs; and one is committed to axiomatic or self-evident principles, such as 'Happiness is good' or 'Promise-keeping is right', in accordance with which one uses these moral words. The 'intuitions' into which moral thinking breaks down are, on this view, rules for the use of the words 'good', 'right', etc., not discernments of the nature of objective reality. It is conceivable that the rules should be other than they are. They vary from age to age, culture to culture. And sometimes an individual person changes his moral principles and uses moral words in accordance with a new set of rules. But all that is involved here is words, and men using them in accordance with rules.

The rationalists were perfectly correct to find an analogy between morals and mathematics. But their Cartesian mentors had taken it for granted that the axioms of the mathematical systems which they used were not simply rules for the use of words, or signs, but ultimate truths about the nature of reality. This was a mistake. Reality may require axioms to be abandoned or altered. Modern mathematicians use other geometries than that of Euclid, constituted by different axioms and, for some purposes, more useful in describing the world or coming to terms with it. The mistake which the rationalists made about the intuitions of morality was simply a 'carry over' from the mistake which the Cartesians had made about mathematics.

If we reject the intuitionist account of the objectivity of moral judgment, it is important to clarify what goes with it and what does not. The contention that we can show men to have knowledge of a metaphysical moral order, comparable to their knowledge of the physical order of nature, must, presumably, go, or find some other ground. But some people appear to think that, if this contention has to be abandoned, morality is evacuated of its significance and seriousness. Moral judgment then becomes no more than the expression of subjective taste or distaste; and it really means nothing any longer to say that man is a moral being. But these conclusions do not necessarily follow.

Moral discourse — whether we regard it as referring to non-natural facts or as registering options — remains *sui generis*. That is to say — if we may conceive of it as a 'language-game' — that the rules of this game are distinctively its own. One need only compare the way in which men talk about what they regard as matters of taste with the way in which they talk about what they regard as moral issues. If a man, having tasted a wine, exclaimed,

'Ugh!', and we said to him, 'Why don't you like it?', he might reply, 'I just don't'; or he might give a reason, such as, 'It's too sweet.' Now, in either case, it would be eccentric on our part, if we tried to argue with him. We should not be likely to pester him for a reason why he did not like the wine, if he said, 'I just don't.' And, if he told us that he did not like it because it was too sweet, it would be rather silly of us to rebuke him for inconsistency because we happened to know that he liked sugar in his tea. But now suppose that this man said, 'Capital punishment is wrong.' It would not be at all eccentric of us to argue with him, if we held another opinion. We should not be behaving oddly if we pressed him for a reason why he thought capital punishment wrong. What would be eccentric is if he were to reply, 'I just do.' Or — if that is putting it rather strongly — we should at least feel that it was not quite playing the game to go around voicing moral judgments and then refusing to give reasons for them. Suppose that he replies to our request for a reason why he thinks capital punishment wrong with some such remark as: 'Because it requires one man to take another man's life and society has no right to ask that of anybody.' It will not now be at all silly to ask him whether he thinks that war is wrong; and if he says that he does not, to accuse him of inconsistency. Faced with such an accusation, he will, no doubt, try to think of some morally relevant respect in which the killing involved in war differs from that which society requires in the case of capital punishment. Enough has been said to show that, in moral discourse, one is expected to give reasons for one's judgments, and to accept the implications of universalising these reasons, as one is not expected to do when merely expressing taste or distaste.[96] There are, no doubt, other defining characteristics of moral discourse besides those noted here.[97] What makes a judgment moral is a question about which a lively discussion is going on at the present time among linguistic philosophers. All it is necessary to bring out for our purpose, however, is that moral discourse does have its own distinctive defining characteristics and cannot logically be reduced to anything other than itself.

Moreover, it is characteristic of man to play this moral language 'game'. Morality is a distinctively human concern. In this sense, man is indeed a moral being. Any account of human life, which ignored the fact that men ask questions, and debate answers, in terms of moral words, such as 'ought', 'right', 'good', would be seriously inadequate.

Some recent Christian authors have suggested — to quote one — that 'Christian morality is indissolubly bound up with the principle of "the objectivity of moral judgments"'; and have even gone so far as to say — to quote another — that, unless moral language has 'objective reference', it is 'impossible . . . to believe in God at all'.[98] If these quotations mean that the Christian faith or ethic stand or fall with philosophical intuitionism, they are surely absurd! The so-called moral argument for the existence of God may do so, but that is another matter. Religious moralists — just like other kinds of moralist, e.g. evolutionists, hedonists, etc. — hold two sorts of view. On the one hand, they believe that something is in fact the case: that X will fulfil the will of God (cf. will conduce to evolution, will produce the greatest happiness of the greatest number, etc.). This belief may, of course, be either true or false. On the other hand, religious moralists, like other kinds of moralist, are committed to a principle of action: We ought to do what conforms to the will of God! (cf. what conduces to evolution, produces the greatest happiness of the greatest number, etc.). Both these sorts of view are logically quite distinct from the philosophical contention that men can be shown to know moral truths by intuition. The relationship between the two sorts of view is, indeed, a matter about which there is animated discussion among modern moral philosophers. It may well be that the logical gap between 'is' and 'ought' — between factual description and moral evaluation — is not so deep and wide as some analytical philosophers have supposed. And it may be that some 'is' statements in religious terms logically imply 'ought' statements. But, whatever opinions ultimately prevail on such matters, they will be concerned with the language men use and the relationship between saying one kind of thing and saying another. The discrediting of intuitionism — if it has been discredited — will have no bearing upon them.

NOTES

References to the works of the intuitionists with whom this study is concerned are given in accordance with the abbreviations below. These works are most easily available to modern readers in L. A. Selby-Bigge's *British Moralists*, vols. i and ii, and wherever possible, the paragraph in Selby-Bigge is referred to along with the original work. In quoting, I have felt free to modernise spelling and punctuation and to exercise my own discretion about the use of italics.

Abbreviations

DNR   Clarke, *A Discourse Concerning the Being and Attributes of God and Obligations of Natural Religion.*
DNV   Butler, *Dissertation Upon the Nature of Virtue.*
EIM   Cudworth, *Treatise on Eternal and Immutable Morality.*
ENP   Hutcheson, *An Essay on the Nature and Conduct of the Passions and Affections.*
EVM   Shaftesbury, *Enquiry Concerning Virtue or Merit.*
FMG   Balguy, *The Foundation of Moral Goodness* (Parts i and ii).
IMG   Hutcheson, *An Inquiry Concerning Moral Good and Evil.*
IMS   Hutcheson, *Illustrations Upon the Moral Sense.*
PRE   Butler, Preface to *Fifteen Sermons.*
RPQ   Price, *Review of the Principal Questions and Difficulties in Morals.*
SB   Selby-Bigge, *British Moralists.*
SER   Butler, *Fifteen Sermons.*

1. Cf. the writings of H. A. Prichard and W. D. Ross.
2. *Leviathan*, I. xv (Everyman edition, p. 74).
3. Cf. B. H. Baumrin's introduction to Selby-Bigge's *British Moralists* (new edition published by Bobbs-Merrill, 1964, pp. xv–xvi).
4. Cf. A. D. Lindsay's *Introduction* to *Leviathan* (Everyman edition, p. xvii); Hume, op. cit. I. xiv.
5. *EVM* II. i. 3 and ii. 1, 2, 3, SB 31–62.
6. *IMG* II. ix, x, SB 106–8.
7. *SER* i, SB 204.
8. *DNR* I. 4, SB 503.
9. *RPQ* viii, SB 712–13; *FMG* i, SB 527.
10. *SER* xii, SB 240; *FMG* i, SB 567.
11. *FMG* i, SB 527.
12. *ENP* i, SB 440.

13. *RPQ* iii, SB 651–3; *SER* xi, SB 229; Price said that desire is *'always* to some particular object different from private pleasure' (italics mine), but Butler did not say or imply this, and seems to have recognised that private pleasure is one possible object of desire. Cf. W. R. Matthews, *Butler's Sermons*, p. 168 n.

14. *Of Human Nature*, ix, SB 909.

15. *SER* i, SB 204 n.

16. Cf. D. D. Raphael, *The Moral Sense*, p. 24.

17. Quoted in J. A. Passmore, *Ralph Cudworth*, p. 53.

18. *FMG* i, SB 559; *DNV*, SB 244; *RPQ* ii, SB 634.

19. Op. cit., p. 56.

20. *IMG* I. iv–vii, II. vii, viii, SB 79–86, 101–5.

21. *IMG* VII. iv, SB 172. I am indebted throughout this Section to A. N. Prior, *Logic and the Basis of Ethics*. I use the term 'naturalist' of one who commits what G. E. Moore called the 'naturalistic fallacy'. Cf. the latter's *Principia Ethica*, p. 10: 'It may be true that all things which are good are *also* something else . . . And it is a fact, that Ethics aims at discovering what are those other properties belonging to all things which are good. But far too many philosophers have thought that when they named those other properties they were actually defining good; that these properties, in fact, were simply not 'other', but absolutely and entirely the same with goodness. This view I propose to call the "naturalistic fallacy". . . .'

22. *Essay Concerning Human Understanding*, II. xxviii, SB 991–7.

23. Op. cit. Cf. Shaftesbury *EVM* I. iii. 2 and Prior, op. cit., pp. 95–96.

24. *RPQ* i, SB 609.

25. Op. cit. I. iii. 18; cf. Prior, op. cit., p. 97.

26. *Leviathan* I. xiv (Everyman edition pp. 66–8); *DNR* I. 1, 7, SB 485–7, 515–16.

27. *EIM* I. ii. 3, SB 816; *RPQ* I. iii, SB 622.

28. Prior, op. cit., p. 99; Moore, op. cit., pp. 9–16.

29. *RPQ* i, SB 586–7; cf. Prior, op. cit., pp. 98–99.

30. *IMS* I, SB 459; *IMG* VII. xii, SB 186.

31. *FMG* i, SB 528–9.

32. Cf. L. Wittgenstein, *Philosophical Investigations*, 43, 421.

33. P. H. Nowell-Smith, *Ethics*, p. 98.

34. *FMG* ii, SB 719.

35. Hare, *The Language of Morals*, p. 85. See Nowell-Smith, op. cit., chap. 3. My purpose here has been simply to show how the argument was turned against the intuitionists. It must not be assumed that the logical impossibility of deducing 'ought' from 'is' has been established beyond all question. A lively debate on this issue is in progress among

moral philosophers. See, *inter alia*, the following papers: G. E. M. Anscombe, 'Modern Moral Philosophy', *Philosophy* xxxiii (1958); P. Foot, 'Moral Beliefs', *Proc. Arist. Soc.* lix (1958–59), 'Moral Arguments', *Mind* lxvii (1958) 'Goodness and Choice', *Proc. Arist. Soc.* supp. vol. lxxxv (1961); D. Z. Phillips and H. O. Mounce, 'On Morality's Having A Point', *Philosophy* xl. (1965); and the papers listed under n. 48 below. See also G. J. Warnock, *Contemporary Moral Philosophy*, sect. vi.

36. *EVM* I. ii. 3 and iii. 2, 3, SB 12, 24–25.

37. *IMG Introd.*, I. i, iv and v, SB 68, 73–74, 79–80; *IMS* I and IV, SB 457, 465.

38. *Theory of Moral Sentiments*, VII. iii. 3, SB 349–51.

39. *IMG* VII. iii, SB 170.

40. *The Moral Sense*, p. 19.

41. *FMG* i, SB 549.

42. *DNR* I. 1, SB 483.

43. *A Treatise of Human Nature* III. i. 1. Selby-Bigge edn, pp. 464 n., 468.

44. *British Moralists*, pp. lv–lvi (1964 edition).

45. *RPQ* vi, SB 692.

46. *RPQ* i and v, SB 590 n., 603, 668; cf. *EIM* IV. ii. 1.

47. *RPQ* v (Raphael's edition, p. 95).

48. For recent discussion on the 'Is–ought' controversy, see J. R. Searle, 'How to Derive "Ought" from "Is" ', *Philosophical Review* lxxiii (1964); M. Black, 'The Gap Between "Is" and "Should" ', ibid.; A. Flew, 'On Not Deriving "Ought" from "Is" ', *Analysis* 24 (1964); W. D. Hudson, 'The "Is–Ought" controversy', *Analysis* 25 (1965); etc.

49. *Dialogues concerning Natural Religion*, ix.

50. *The Right and the Good*, pp. 121–2; *Foundations of Ethics*, p. 52.

51. Op. cit., p. 41 (italics mine).

52. *DNV*, SB 249.

53. *DNV*, SB 244; cf. *RPQ* ii, SB 634; but Price considers the feeling of the heart to be parasitic upon the understanding's intuition.

54. *SER* ii, SB 216.

55. See *DNV*, SB 245, on intention and character as objects of moral judgment.

56. *PRE*, SB 200.

57. *PRE*, SB 194; *SER* i, SB 206.

58. *PRE*, *SER* i and ii, SB 190, 198, 204, 205 n., 206, 216, 218. The terms 'passion', 'appetite', 'affection', in this analysis do not appear to have been used completely interchangeably. It would have seemed odd to Butler, as to us, to call hunger a passion, or desire for esteem an appetite. Cf. A. Duncan-Jones, *Butler's Moral Philosophy*, p. 45.

59. *PRE*, SB 191.
60. *DNV*, SB 244 n.
61. *SER* ii, SB 219.
62. *SER* iii, SB 223; *SER* ii, SB 212–13.
63. *IMS passim*, SB 447–70. Selby-Bigge does not give the whole of *Illustrations* and, to follow Hutcheson's argument fully, the reader will need to get a copy of the whole work.
64. *IMS* I, SB 454 (parenthesis mine).
65. *FMG* i and ii, SB 559, 565, 732.
66. *RPQ* i, SB 585; *IMS* i and iv, SB 458, 459, 465, 466; on emotivism and prescriptivism, see G. J. Warnock, *Contemporary Moral Philosophy*.
67. *DNR* I. 3, SB 491.
68. See W. Wollaston, *The Religion of Nature Delineated* i, SB 1023–60.
69. *Treatise*, III. i. 1 (Selby-Bigge edition, p. 462 n.).
70. *FMG* i, SB 550–3; *RPQ* vi, SB 693–6.
71. *EVM* I. ii. 3, SB 13.
72. *RPQ* viii, SB 700–4; cf. *IMS* I, SB 450. (See Section IX (iii) below on the distinction between absolute and practical virtue.)
73. Op. cit.
74. *IMG* III. viii, SB 121.
75. For the two views, cf. H. Sidgwick, *Outlines of the History of Ethics*, p. 203, and N. H. G. Robinson, *The Claim of Morality*, pp. 47–48.
76. *DNV*, SB 245.
77. *DNV*, SB 249.
78. *EVM* II. i. 1, SB 26–28; *SER* xi, SB 239.
79. *EIM* I. ii. 4, SB 817.
80. *DNR* I. 4, SB 498–505.
81. *RPQ* vii.
82. Cf. W. D. Ross, *Foundations of Ethics*, p. 272.
83. Cf. E. F. Carritt, *Ethical and Political Thinking*, p. 102.
84. *RPQ* vii (D. D. Raphael's edition, p. 167).
85. Cf. W. D. Ross, *The Right and the Good*, p. 28, and *Foundations of Ethics*, p. 86; C. D. Broad, 'Some of the Main Problems in Ethics', *Philosophy* xxi (1946), p. 117; for criticism of this view, see P. F. Strawson, 'Ethical Intuitionism', *Philosophy* xxiv (1949).
86. Op. cit., p. 29.
87. *RPQ* vii (Raphael's edition, p. 170).
88. *Existentialism and Humanism* (English translation by P. Mairet, p. 37).
89. *Human Society in Ethics and Politics*, p. 38.
90. *RPQ* vii (Raphael's edition, pp. 170 ff.).

91. Cf. E. F. Carritt, op. cit., p. 14 n.; *RPQ* viii, SB 699.
92. Cf. Sidgwick, op. cit., p. 203.
93. H. A. Prichard, *Moral Obligation*, p. 24; W. D. Ross, *Foundations of Ethics*, p. 150.
94. *The Problem of Knowledge*, pp. 33 and 82.
95. J. O. Urmson, 'Saints and Heroes', *Essays in Moral Philosophy*, ed. A. I. Melden, p. 207; P. Edwards, *The Logic of Moral Discourse*, p. 100.
96. Cf. W. D. Hudson, 'On the Alleged Objectivity of Moral Judgment', *Mind* lxxi (1962).
97. See also G. J. Warnock, op. cit.
98. See R. Corkey, *A Philosophy of Christian Morals for Today*, p. 32, and H. P. Owen, *The Moral Argument for Christian Theism*, p. 12.

BIBLIOGRAPHY

I. Texts

Balguy, J. *The Foundation of Moral Goodness*, parts i and ii (1728, 1729.)

Butler, J. *Fifteen Sermons* (London, 1726).
Dissertation upon the Nature of Virtue (London, 1736).

Clarke, S. *A Discourse Concerning the Being and Attributes of God, and Obligations of Natural Religion, etc.* (1706).

Cudworth, R. *Treatise on Eternal and Immutable Morality* (London, 1731).

Hutcheson, F. *An Inquiry Concerning Moral Good and Evil* (London, 1725).
An Essay on the Nature and Conduct of the Passions and Affections, (1728).
Illustrations Upon the Moral Sense (1728).

Price, R. *Review of the Principal Questions and Difficulties in Morals* (1758).

Shaftesbury, Earl of, *Enquiry Concerning Virtue or Merit* (1699).

Extracts from the above works will be found in L. A. Selby-Bigge, *British Moralists*, vols. i and ii (Oxford, 1897). These two volumes are bound together in a paperback edition published by Bobbs-Merrill (New York, 1964).

II. Some books in which Eighteenth-Century Intuitionists are Discussed

Aqvist, L. *The Moral Philosophy of Richard Price* (Uppsala, 1960).

Broad, C. D. *Five Types of Ethical Theory* (London, 1930).

Duncan-Jones, A. *Butler's Moral Philosophy* (Pelican, 1952).

Hospers, J. *Human Conduct* (New York, 1961).

Kemp, J. *Reason, Action and Morality* (London, 1964).

72

Lillie, W. *An Introduction to Ethics* (London, 1948).

Mackenzie, J. S. *A Manual of Ethics* (6th edn) (London, 1929).

Martineau, J. *Types of Ethical Theory* (Oxford, 1901).

Matthews, W. R. *Introduction* to his edition of Butler's *Sermons* (London, 1914).

Passmore, J. A. *Ralph Cudworth* (Cambridge, 1951).

Prior, A. N. *Logic and the Basis of Ethics* (Oxford, 1949).

Rashdall, H. *The Theory of Good and Evil* (Oxford, 1907).

Raphael, D. D. *The Moral Sense* (London, 1947).

Introduction to his edition of Price's *Review* (Oxford, 1948).

Robinson, N. H. G. *The Claim of Morality* (London, 1952).

Rogers, R. A. P. *A Short History of Ethics* (London, 1945).

Selby-Bigge, L. A. *Introduction* to his *British Moralists* (Oxford, 1897).

Sidgwick, H. *Outlines of the History of Ethics* (London, 1931).

III. SOME MODERN WORKS IN WHICH ETHICAL INTUITIONISM IS EXPOUNDED OR CRITICISED

Carritt, E. F. *Ethical and Political Thinking* (Oxford, 1947).

Edwards, P. *The Logic of Moral Discourse* (Glencoe, Illinois, 1955).

Ewing, A. C. *Ethics* (London, 1953).

Frankena, W. K. *Ethics* (Englewood Cliffs, N.J., 1963).

Hare, R. M. *The Language of Morals* (Oxford, 1952).

Moore, G. E. *Principia Ethica* (Cambridge, 1903).

Ethics (London, 1912).

Nowell-Smith, P. H. *Ethics* (London, 1954).

Prichard, H. A. *Moral Obligation* (Oxford, 1949).

Ross, W. D. *The Right and the Good* (Oxford, 1930).

The Foundations of Ethics (Oxford, 1939).

Warnock, G. J. *Contemporary Moral Philosophy* (London, 1967).

INDEX